RX

Diversity
Programming for
Digital Youth

Recent Titles in the
Children's and Young Adult Literature Reference Series
Catherine Barr, Series Editor

Literature Links to American History, 7–12: Resources to Enhance and Entice
Lynda G. Adamson

Literature Links to American History, K–6: Resources to Enhance and Entice
Lynda G. Adamson

Celebrating Cuentos: Promoting Latino Children's Literature and Literacy in
Classrooms and Libraries
Jamie Campbell Naidoo, Editor

The Family in Literature for Young Readers: A Resource Guide for Use with
Grades 4 to 9
John T. Gillespie

Best Books for High School Readers, Grades 9–12: Supplement to the Second Edition
Catherine Barr

Best Books for Middle School and Junior High Readers, Grades 6–9:
Supplement to the Second Edition
Catherine Barr

Rainbow Family Collections: Selecting and Using Children's Books with Lesbian,
Gay, Bisexual, Transgender, and Queer Content
Jamie Campbell Naidoo

A to Zoo: Subject Access to Children's Picture Books, Supplement to the 8th Edition
Rebecca L. Thomas

Best Books for Children: Preschool Through Grade 6, Supplement to the 9th Edition
Catherine Barr

Best Books for Middle School and Junior High Readers, Grades 6–9: Third Edition
Catherine Barr

Best Books for High School Readers, Grades 9–12: Third Edition
Catherine Barr

A to Zoo: Subject Access to Children's Picture Books, Ninth Edition
Rebecca L. Thomas

Diversity Programming for Digital Youth

PROMOTING CULTURAL COMPETENCE
IN THE CHILDREN'S LIBRARY

Jamie Campbell Naidoo

Children's and Young Adult Literature Reference
Catherine Barr, Series Editor

AN IMPRINT OF ABC-CLIO, LLC
Santa Barbara, California • Denver, Colorado • Oxford, England

Library of Congress Cataloging-in-Publication Data

Naidoo, Jamie Campbell.
  Diversity programming for digital youth : promoting cultural competence in the
children's library / Jamie Campbell Naidoo.
    pages cm. — (Children's and young adult literature reference)
  Includes bibliographical references and index.
  ISBN 978-1-61069-487-2 (hardback) — ISBN 978-1-61069-488-9 (ebook)
  1. Children's libraries—Services to minorities—United States. 2. Children's
libraries—Reference services—Data processing. 3. Children's libraries—Collection
development—United States. 4. Library outreach programs—United States.
5. Library information networks—United States. 6. Multiculturalism—United
States. 7. Libraries and families—United States. 8. Libraries and community—
United States. 9. Libraries and minorities—United States. 10. Internet and children.
11. Digital media. I. Title.
  Z718.1.N35 2014
  027.62'5—dc23   2014011833

ISBN: 978-1-61069-487-2
EISBN: 978-1-61069-488-9

18 17 16 15 14   1 2 3 4 5

This book is also available on the World Wide Web as an eBook.
Visit www.abc-clio.com for details.

Libraries Unlimited
An Imprint of ABC-CLIO, LLC

ABC-CLIO, LLC
130 Cremona Drive, P.O. Box 1911
Santa Barbara, California 93116-1911

This book is printed on acid-free paper ∞
Manufactured in the United States of America

Dedication

In memory of Eliza Dresang
for her memorable "Radical Change" that led many children's
librarians to consider the possibilities of technology, cultural
competence, and children's books.

To Cen Campbell
for advocating "Rousing Change" in library land and leading the
charge to embrace digital media in the children's library.

Acknowledgments

Behind every book is a support team of editors, assistants, and advocates.
I wish to thank my colleagues for their support as I worked on this book
and my better half who never seems to tire of listening to me rant and rave
about children's media and cultural diversity.

Barbara Ittner at Libraries Unlimited has been extremely gracious
and patient in encouraging and overseeing the publication process. A
special thanks also goes to Christine McNaull for her assistance with designing, proofing, and typesetting the book, and to my graduate assistant
Christie Bethard for her many hours helping me locate multicultural children's apps. Above all, my deepest gratitude goes to Catherine Barr for
her unending patience, resourcefulness, humor, and kindness through yet
another book project. I'm glad you haven't tired of me yet!

Thanks to all the children's librarians who are doing a fabulous job
connecting digital natives with high-quality print and digital materials that
celebrate cultural diversity. Sincere appreciation goes to Cen Campbell,
Betsy Diamant-Cohen, Marianne Martens, and Allison Tran for your
willingness to share your expertise. Finally, I am thankful to Sarah Park
Dahlen for beginning this project with me and contributing as much as
possible through her exciting life changes.

Contents

I

Cultural Competence, Children, and the Library

II

Digital Media, Children, and the Library

III

Putting It All Together

Connecting with Today's Diverse Children via Literature and New Digital Media in the Children's Library

Do e-books and other digital media supersede the printed word? Will using new digital media in library programming for children and their families interfere with the healthy development of young children? Children have enough exposure to the screen throughout their waking hours, shouldn't librarians promote the use of printed materials? Will the use of digital media actually create a larger digital divide rather than bringing disparate cultural groups together? All of these questions are important to consider as we begin the journey to understanding and exploiting the potential for using new digital media in children's library programming to build bridges of understanding.

Guernsey and Levin (2012) observe, "With the advent of new technologies, we are at an opportune moment for realizing digital media to support parents, educators, and children in building the next generation's reading skills. But technology's potential to be a game changer will not be reached unless technology is tapped to provide vital new supports for parents and educators. At its best, the technology complements the work of trained teachers, [librarians,] and parents. It doesn't replace it." (par. 7) In a recent blog posting a respected information science scholar suggests that libraries as we currently know them are passé because we are not embracing the digital media around us. He notes that digital natives and society at large increasingly demand new media experiences in order to actively participate in life-long learning. He calls for librarians—the stodgy, stick-in-the-mud folks that we are—to cease with book pushing, get over ourselves, and embrace the new digital media that spring forth daily. He also postulates that libraries are becoming irrelevant as many other public agencies and resources are duplicating our efforts.

Based on this scholar's comments, it would seem that he has not been in a children's library lately. Indeed, public and school libraries across the nation are harnessing the power of media to engage children from a myriad of socioeconomic backgrounds with both print and digital media on a daily basis. Through digital storytimes and makerspaces, children and their caregivers embrace new technology and new media while also celebrating *bookjoy*—the joy that comes from reading and sharing books with family and friends. Other public agencies may provide childcare or educational services and may include access to digital media, but no other public agency does this freely to the masses. No other public agency employs trained professionals who are cognizant of childhood development practices, educational programming, and the best ways to connect digital natives with books in all their formats.

Children's librarians have been on the cutting edge of the information field since the beginning. One only needs to look at early passionate pioneers such as Anne Carroll Moore, Pura Belpré, Augusta Baker, Mary Frances Isom, Charlemae Rollins, and Mary Huffer, who looked beyond the hollow warnings of scholars and fellow librarians in the field and broke down institutional and social barriers by opening library doors to children and culturally diverse populations during times when libraries were hallowed, stoic places of learning not meant for the likes of children, English language learners, or non-white individuals. Early pioneers bucked social norms and convention to create a richer, freer informational environment.

In the past, naysayers also predicted the end of libraries with the advent of "new media" such as records, films, audiobooks, and the Internet. However, just as the early passionate pioneer librarians embraced change, later children's librarians adopted the new media of their time, creating multimedia programs for children and their families. As technology changed, film strips were replaced with video cassettes and then DVDs and later streaming video. Yet passionate librarians held onto their belief in *bookjoy,* marrying high-quality literature with the new digital media of the time. Today, passionate librarians such as Cen Campbell, Gretchen Caserotti, Genesis Hansen, Claudia Haines, Kiera Parrott, Kelsey Cole, Emily Scherrer, Jennifer Gal, Kate Lucey, and Melissa Della Pena, to name a few, embrace the use of digital apps for tablets in their children's programming, creating high-tech, high-touch, book-enriched, and developmentally appropriate experiences for children and their families.

With all this change and embracing of new digital media within the history of children's librarianship it is clear that brick and mortar libraries are here to stay, although outreach programs may be virtual or within the community. But there is one bridge that still needs to be built. Despite the current inclusion of digital apps and other digital media in library programming, many digital storytimes and other programs embracing digital media do not examine or celebrate cultural diversity. Almost fifty years ago, Nancy Larrick (1965) called for an end to the "all-white world" of children's books. Today, many digital media and apps are either Eurocentric or virtually culturally generic. All children need to develop their understanding of their own cultures and the cultures of those around them. The opportunity to pair high-quality culturally diverse literature with digital apps, digital picture books, and other digital media is ripe for the picking. It is my expectation that this book can serve as a catalyst for book-enriched, high-tech, high-touch children's programs that promote cultural competence *and* bookjoy.

Organization of the Book

This book begins with a discussion of culture and cultural competence, describing the role of children's media and the library in the process of developing cultural competence. Next we explore how to plan culturally competent programs. With this foundation in place, we define and discuss the use of digital media with young children and describe how contemporary librarians are using digital media in storytimes. Then, we examine the idea of planning culturally competent library programs that incorporate digital media to provide opportunities for new literacy explorations. Finally, we provide a few sample program ideas and book-digital media pairings to demonstrate how print and digital materials can be used together to promote cultural connections in the children's library.

Digital media usage with young children in classrooms, libraries, and home—and attitudes regarding these interactions—is changing at an exponential rate. New reports appear almost monthly and librarian and educator blogs and journals publish new information at an exciting pace. Truly this is a "hot topic" in the field of children's librarianship and early childhood education. As such, I have tried to capture as much of this conversation as possible. Whenever I set one chapter aside to begin another during the writing of this book, something new and exciting would happen and I would go back to update the previous chapter. At some point, we have to step back and look at the big picture. This is what I have tried to do. Invariably I may have missed an important discussion that has occurred since writing a particular chapter; but I have provided recommendations for where librarians and educators can go to keep current on the most up-to-date information. It is my hope that I have provided the foundation for carefully and objectively thinking about the use of digital media in the children's library, particularly the use of these media to promote cultural understanding and connections. Certainly librarians can choose to only use print materials to help children and their families develop cultural competence, but the possibilities are greatly expanded with the inclusion of digital media.

Throughout this book I have recommended various digital apps and other digital media. As this landscape is changing rapidly, a wonderful app I have recommended may not be available when a librarian is ready to plan a particular program. If this is the case, librarians are encouraged to use the various recommended review sources as well as the recommendations for evaluating the cultural content of digital media to find a replacement app. At times this book shies away from recommending a specific app or digital media product to provide space for librarians to find their own favorite. Similarly, as there are many, many resources available for locating high-quality culturally diverse children's literature, I have selected only a few examples of titles to use in cultural programs and provided guidance for librarians and educators to find more in the Bibliography. Finally, considering the fluid nature of digital media, I have chosen to provide only a selection of print and digital media pairings to use for promoting cultural competence among children and families. Librarians can use the examples as a guide to create their own unique and exciting pairings to plan diversity programming for digital youth.

References

Guernsey, Lisa, and Michael Levine. (December 13, 2012). "Educational Apps Alone Won't Teach Your Child to Read." *Slate.* Accessed November 21, 2013, at http://www.slate.com/blogs/future_tense/2012/12/13/kids_apps_and_ebooks_can_t_teach_them_to_read_without_parent_and_teacher.html.

Larrick, Nancy. "The All-White World of Children's Books," *Saturday Review* (11 Sept. 1965): 63–65.

I

Cultural Competence, Children, and the Library

Chapter 1

Cultural Competence in the Library

> Stories matter. Many stories matter. Stories have been used to dispossess and to malign, but stories can also be used to empower and to humanize. Stories can break the dignity of a people, but stories can also repair that broken dignity (Adichie, 2009, quote 564).

> The single story creates stereotypes, and the problem with stereotypes is not that they are untrue, but that they are incomplete. They make one story become the only story (Adichie, 2009, quote 558).

Passionate, culturally competent librarians are the foundation for change within the library profession. They are believers, schemers, and dreamers. Passionate librarians are literacy advocates who firmly believe that all children and their families should have access to high-quality materials designed especially for them. These same librarians understand the power of both print and digital children's media to shape a child's view of the world and to build bridges of understanding. Culturally competent librarians dream of a day when all children from all cultural backgrounds are validated with authentic representations in the books, movies, digital apps, and other new media that they encounter. Most of all, passionate librarians are schemers, taking every opportunity to network with other literacy professionals (teachers, authors, illustrators, nonprofit organizations and associations, etc.) to develop and implement outreach services and programs that bring together children and families from diverse cultural backgrounds to celebrate many children, many cultures, many voices, and many languages.

Throughout this chapter we will conceptualize the idea of cultural competence in the library and how it can be cultivated in librarians, children, and their families. Part of this journey is examining the influence that a single story or a series of culturally inaccurate stories can have on the identity and social development of children. Stories can be found in traditional print materials for children or in newer digital formats. Regardless of the package (book or digital device) used for delivering a story's message, children are greatly influenced by the stories they encounter in homes, classrooms, and libraries.

Culture and Cultural Competence

According to Clifford Geertz (1973), *culture* can be defined as "the shared patterns that set the tone, character and quality of people's lives" (p. 216). Ethnicity, race, family composition, ancestry, ability, sexual orientation, socioeconomic status, language fluency, citizenship status, religious preference, age, gender expression, education level, and domicile are all aspects of a person's culture. Sonia Nieto (1999) explains that the idea of culture is quite complex, going beyond foods, festivals, and folklore to include daily experiences influenced by social, historical, and political facets of a particular locale, region, nation, and so forth. She also suggests that culture is heavily influenced by the dominant power within a particular area and is socially constructed from childhood by the belief systems of this dominant power. Children experience culture as a by-product of their families' values and practices and in their daily interactions in schools, churches and synagogues, playgrounds, and other places throughout the neighborhood. Carlos Cortés (2002) calls these cultural influences a *societal curriculum*, meant to represent the "real-world" education that takes place outside the classroom. A societal curriculum can have a bearing on how a child interacts with others within and outside his or her culture. Cortés further subdivides the societal curriculum according to the various means by which society influences a child's understanding of culture and the world. These include the immediate curriculum (family, peers, and community), the institutional curriculum (non-school institutions such as libraries, churches and synagogues, community organizations, etc.), the serendipitous curriculum (unplanned, individualized experiences with other cultures), and the media curriculum (news, film, books, radio, online games, Internet, and so forth). All of these different curricula are continuously influencing children's cultures throughout their entire lives.

"From childhood, we learn to look at people's differences primarily through cultural or racial identities—e.g., this is an Asian family, she is African American, they are Italian. Each cultural/ethnic identification suggests a set of generalized expectations covering religion, styles of communication, attitudes about family relationships, and types of careers or businesses" (Tanner et al., 1996, p. 1). These generalized behavioral expectations are called social scripts and define how we view our actions and those of people from other cultures. Since social scripts vary from culture to culture, misunderstandings can occur when one person's social script does not match that of another person. For instance, in some cultures it is believed that the community raises the child. As such, parents from that culture may allow their child to roam around a department store or library with the expectation that the greater community will watch over that child and keep him safe. Someone from outside that culture may perceive this practice as negligence on the part of the parents, believing that young children should be supervised by an adult at all times. The two cultures have different notions on child rearing practices that are defined by their divergent social scripts.

According to Sandra Ríos-Balderama (2006), there are four cultural characteristics that can influence how we interact with one another and the behavioral expectations that we hold in particular situations. These are:

Identity: Individual and Collective

Americans (from the United States) value individuality, which is closely associated with independence, privacy, autonomy, and an ability to determine one's path in the world. Other cultures value the collective—that is the communal or familial group of support that one proudly depends on for regular social gatherings, advisory, and shared decision-making.

Contexts: Low and High

For cultures that value a high context it is the meaning, setting, and how something is said that is important. Ritual and formality can be important. In low-context cultures, one might be quick, direct, and to the point. Informality of events will not diminish the content. To use a programming example—how you welcome people from a high-context culture is just as important as the content; therefore many ethnic cultural celebrations include food, refreshments (at minimum), and decorations. A low-context person may find this effort "too much." Many Americans tend to value low-context situations.

Authority: Small and Large Power Distance

Americans value a small power distance. We value egalitarianism but we are realistic that hierarchies exist, particularly in library organizations. We do have some respect for hierarchy but we believe that, if need be, we have access to "the top" because it is our right. We value questioning, debate, and critical thinking. Large power distance cultures show deference to the person in authority. Whether that person earned that status or was given that status at birth, a level of deference and distance is associated with respectful behavior.

Time: Linear and Fluid

We in the United States tend to be linear and look at the present, but more to the future. Time is limited, precious, and highly guarded. Cultures that look at time in a fluid manner look at the "right time." The time to start a gathering or join a gathering may be when everyone is present, when the elder has entered the room, and/or when people "can get there." Time is also related to high context. Setting the tone takes more time. Getting to the point takes less time. For a high-context culture, "taking time" is investing in the relationship rather than limiting time or speeding through it. For some cultures, time may also include the past. In the United States you will often hear bicultural people or people-of-color thanking those "who went before" or those "whose shoulders we stand on." In regard to the saying "that was then, this is now"—the contrast is that for many other cultures "then" is integrated with "now" and ancestors are still part of the family. Sometimes this last piece is associated with being from a "premodern" culture. (Ríos-Balderama, 2006, 6–7)

Each of these cultural characteristics drives how we interact with each other and with the larger world. As librarians it is imperative that we understand culture and the role that it plays in our daily lives. Culture influences how we plan programs, develop collections, and create services.

Understanding how particular cultural groups perceive time, authority, identity, and context is integral to building a children's library that nurtures and promotes cultural understanding. Being able to conceptualize the role that culture plays in daily interactions helps librarians recognize the importance of cultural competence in the library.

Patti Montiel-Overall (2009), one of the foremost experts on *cultural competence* in libraries, defines the concept as "the ability to recognize the significance of culture in one's own life and in the lives of others; and to come to know and respect diverse cultural backgrounds and characteristics through interaction with individuals from diverse linguistic, cultural, and socioeconomic groups; and to fully integrate the culture of diverse groups into services, work, and institutions in order to enhance the lives of both those being served by the library profession and those engaged in service" (pp. 189–190). Cultural competence applies to everyone: librarians, children, and caregivers. A librarian must develop his or her own cultural competence or be on the road to developing cultural competence before he or she can plan library programs that promote cultural competence among children and families. Achieving cultural competence is a process that happens over time and is at the far end of a continuum that runs from *cultural incapacity* (inability to understand and appreciate cultures) to *cultural blindness* (wearing "rose-colored glasses" or refusing to acknowledge the culture of other people, claiming that we are all the same) to *partial cultural competence* (awareness of one's own culture and the contributions of other cultures) and finally to *proficient cultural competence* (awareness of one's own culture, the contributions of other cultures, and the ability to interact with other individuals from diverse cultures and to understand how cultures are integrated together within society) (Montiel-Overall, 2009; Ríos-Balderama, 2006; Abilock, 2006). While it is beneficial to society for everyone to be culturally competent, some individuals may never reach proficient cultural competence. Since individualized experiences and perspectives shape our understanding and acceptance of the world around us, the journey to full cultural competence is a unique experience that can be positively influenced by opportunities to interact with culturally and linguistically diverse persons through activities, celebrations, and programs that facilitate intercultural connections.

Children who exhibit cultural competence are able to link their cultural experiences, native languages, and personal heritages with those around them and the larger world. The Metiri Group and North Central Regional Educational Laboratory (NCREL) observe that children who are on the way to developing cultural competence exhibit the following characteristics. They

- understand that culture impacts their behavior and beliefs, and the behavior and beliefs of others.
- are aware of specific cultural beliefs, values, and sensibilities that might affect the way that they and others think or behave.
- appreciate and accept diverse beliefs, appearances, and lifestyles.
- are aware that historical knowledge is constructed, and is therefore shaped by personal, political, and social forces.
- know the history of both mainstream and non-mainstream American cultures, and understand that these histories have an impact today.
- are able to take the perspective of non-mainstream groups when learning about historical events.
- know about major historical events of other nations and understand that these events impact behaviors, beliefs, and relationships with others.
- are aware of the similarities between groups of different cultural backgrounds and acceptant of differences between them.
- understand the dangers of stereotyping and other biases; are aware of and sensitive to issues of racism and prejudice.
- are bilingual or multilingual, or working toward these proficiencies.
- can communicate, interact, and work positively with individuals from other cultural groups.
- understand how the use of technology and the Internet impacts worldviews.
- use technology in order to communicate with individuals and access resources from other cultures.
- are familiar with existing cultural norms of technology environments, and are able to interact successfully in such environments. (Metiri and NCREL, par. 1)

Using various print and digital collections in the library and programming activities, librarians can provide opportunities for children to develop the skills necessary to achieve cultural competence. At the same time, librarians can help caregivers and other family members work toward attaining cultural competence by planning intergenerational library programs that include extended family members in storytelling, read-alouds, hands-on activities, and so forth. Creative librarians can rely on the expertise of caregivers and other adults from a cultural group to assist in planning activities that facilitate learning about their culture. By participating in the program planning and execution, adults strengthen their own cultural competence development as they work to find ways to share their culture with others from outside their cultural group in meaningful ways that will foster intercultural connections.

Culture and Children's Print and Digital Media

Numerous scholars have written about the power of culturally diverse literature to open windows and doors to understanding about diverse cultures or provide mirrors reflecting one's own culture. Cortés' (2002) media curriculum described above further underscores the influence that print and digital media can have on the cultural development of a child. Whenever children interact with a book, digital app, ebook, film, or other piece of media, they consume the social messages about culture imbedded within the media. If a librarian, educator, or other caregiver does not point out stereotypes in this media, then children internalize the messages as fact. Over time this consistent reinforcement of stereotypes can lead to negative identity development among children whose cultures are being stereotyped, or can indoctrinate children from outside the culture with misinformation that will be with them the rest of their lives or until the information is challenged by way of other media or external social curricula as described by Cortés.

To better understand the cultural meaning that children glean from print and digital texts we can turn to Louise Rosenblatt's reader response theory and Lev Vygotsky's sociocultural theory. The foundation of sociocultural theory suggests that environments, which are socially constructed by various outside factors or social curricula, mediate human minds—how we approach a problem, interact with others from within and outside our culture, and so forth. Vygotsky (1978; 1986) emphasizes the importance of language and culture in a child's construction of meaning, explaining that children use expressive media (books, digital media, film, etc.) to relate to their social contextual surroundings. Ostensibly, children use their experiences, and images of specific cultures in the media and throughout society, to develop an understanding of how society views that particular culture. When responding to a piece of print or digital media, each reader has a unique experience governed by their own experiences, their culture, the environment, and the work itself (Rosenblatt, 1938). This explains why two individuals can read the same book or interact with the same piece of digital media and have two diverse responses to the information being presented. For instance, let's imagine that a children's librarian has just finished a storytime program on families. He has read multiple books including *Monday Is One Day* (Levine & Hector, 2011) to a group of children from diverse backgrounds. Jasmine might raise her hand after hearing the story and remark that she likes the story because it reminds her of the special moments she spends with her two dads. On the other hand, Micah might connect with the child in the story who lives with grandparents since he just came back from a long visit to his Granny's house. José responds positively to the images of the child with a single parent because his family is composed of himself and his dad. Finally, Kiki's family has just moved to the suburban library community from a largely urban area; as such she relates to the children living in the urban context as this element comprises her most recent experiences. All of these children hear the same story but will respond differently based on their cultural backgrounds and life experiences. Theo, a child who has heard from his parents and the news media that gay families are bad, may react negatively to the same image that Jasmine finds comforting. If he is exposed over time to other media that normalize the experiences of Jasmine's family, then Theo may come to understand that Jasmine doesn't have a "bad" family, just one that is different from his and as equally valid. However, if Theo is never introduced to other stories with gay families, then it is unlikely that he will grow to understand and appreciate Jasmine's family composition. Moreover, if he continues to hear news stories or family conversations that demonize gay families, then he will begin to develop negative feelings toward Jasmine and her family.

How does this apply to librarians? When choosing books for the library collection or to use in library programs, it is imperative that children's librarians select materials that represent a wide range of perspectives and cultures. Opportunities should be provided for children and caregivers to hear stories and interact with characters whose lives and experiences are different from their own. Virginia Walter (2010) observes that "American cultural hegemony is so strong that it is much more likely that a child living in France, Korea, or Kenya will read a book about the United States than that an American child will read a book that originated in one of those countries" (p. 69). Our children need a global perspective on the world in order to develop cultural competence and move beyond their microworlds. They need to hear more than one story once a year about a particular cultural group. Too often librarians rely on culturally sanitized books for storytime programs and relegate cultural explorations and discussions to holidays and specialized months: Native American Heritage Month, Asian Pacific American Heritage Month, and so on. If a child is only introduced to books representing his culture one time a year, then what messages is he internalizing? That the librarian thinks he's not important or that his culture is not important. What if this one-month talent show of Native American cultures includes books that stereotype, demean, or provide misinformation? What is the Native American child internalizing and what are his classmates learning? At the same time, if children are never exposed to the lives of children from around the world, then how can we expect them to successfully function in a culturally pluralistic world?

Global understanding is part of proficient cultural competence. Children who exhibit global understanding can acknowledge how cultural differences as well as personal decisions impact national participation at a global level. These children also have a sense of social justice and engage in local, national, or international service projects that reach out to their counterparts around the world. Through the use of digital media these children are able to successfully interact with children from other countries and cultures. The road to developing global understanding and achieving cultural competence can start in the children's library by way of collections and programs that include *global literature*—an inclusive term meant to represent multicultural literature as well as literature published around the world. According to Judi Moreillon (2013), "cultural literatures have become essential resources for engaging in meaningful, relevant literacy learning. Just as multicultural literature has the potential to increase cultural competence about nonwhite Americans, international children's and young adult literature has a key role to play in developing our young people's global understandings" (p. 35).

Libraries and Cultural Competence

Tate (1971) acknowledges that the "librarian's role may be foreseen as that of helping to open the book of life to children and young people while recognizing their different cultural advantages" (p. 398). A library fully engaged in promoting cultural competence through collections, services, and programs provides numerous opportunities for children and their families to learn about their cultures, diverse cultures in society, and the importance of empowering relationships among the cultures. This sentiment is

Jella Lepman: A Pioneer Promoting
Cultural Competence in the Children's Library

In 1936 Jewish children's author and journalist Jella Lepman fled Germany with her family to escape Hitler's regime. Later, in 1945, she returned under the direction of the U.S. government to help establish a re-education program for German citizens. She quickly redefined her job to build bridges of cultural understanding between German children and the rest of the world. A dynamic, tireless advocate for the power of children's books to foster cross-cultural understanding, Lepman opened the first international exhibition of books for children and young people a year later in Munich. The exhibition included books from twenty countries. Three years later she opened the International Youth Library, designed to offer cultural programs to children and provide opportunities for them to connect with other cultures through global literature. All the while, she traveled the world seeking publisher donations to the library, bringing with her the message that children's books could promote cultural competence.

In 1951 she organized a children's literature congress entitled International Understanding Through Children's Books with the purpose of raising awareness about the role of global children's literature in promoting peace and understanding. Approximately 250 authors, illustrators, librarians, educators, book publishers, professors, and others interested in children's literature attended the congress. From the dialog at the conference emerged the idea of a professional association that would help promote the idea of books as messengers of peace and support the opportunities for children around the world to have access to high-quality literature. In 1953 this international association was founded in Zurich as the International Board on Books for Young People (IBBY). With Lepman's help, the organization grew, inaugurating the international Hans Christian Andersen Prize for children's literature in 1956 and Bookbird, the organization's international journal of children's literature study, in 1957. Almost a

echoed by Larson (2011) who notes, "Library programs and celebrations must promote books that reflect our national plurality and the many cultures represented in our communities" (par. 6). Since language is part of a child's culture, it is essential that libraries reinforce multilingualism by offering programs that introduce children to a variety of languages and encourage them to play with language learning and acquisition. In a culturally

decade later, in 1966, she established International Children's Book Day on April 2nd, Hans Christian Andersen's birthday.

Lepman truly understood the role that media plays in the lives of young children and was a visionary in promoting cultural competence in the children's library and beyond. "Through the . . . International Youth Library in Munich and . . . through the foundation of the International Board on Books for Young People (IBBY), Jella Lepman opened wide the doors to mutual understanding among people in every country who care about the education, development, and future of their children. She created sanctuaries of peace, brotherhood and love among people, focusing on the role and significance of children's books [as messengers of peace]" (Bernbaum, 1992, pp. 9–10).

Additional information about Lepman and the IYL can be found in the following resources:

A Bridge of Children's Books: The Inspiring Autobiography of a Remarkable Woman. Jella Lepman. Dublin: The O'Brien Press, 2002. (Originally published in German in 1964 by Fischer as *Die Kinderbuchbrücke.*)

Books for Children of the World: The Story of Jella Lepman. Sydelle Pearl and Danlyn Iantorno. Gretna, LA: Pelican Publishing, 2007.

"Author Spotlight: Jella Lepman (1891–1970)." Eva-Maria Metcalf. *Bookbird* 40, 3 (2002): 6–10.

"The Role of Children's Libraries in Developing a Multicultural Dialogue." Jutta Reusch. *Knjižnica* 53, 1–2 (2009): 209–219.

"The International Youth Library Today and Tomorrow." Barbara Sharioth. *Bookbird* 40, 3 (2002): 11–15.

Mrs. Lepman: Give Us Books, Give Us Wings. Lioba Betten. Munich: R. Kovar, 1992.

International Youth Library/Internationale Jugendbibliothek Official Website. Available: http://www.ijb.de/files/english/Hme_1/Page01.htm.

International Board on Books for Young People Official Website. Available: http://www.ibby.org/

Figure 1.1: Jella Lepman: A Pioneer Promoting Cultural Competence in the Children's Library

competent library program, librarians share books about global cultures and introduce children to world languages through read-alouds in multiple languages or songs designed to teach learning of a second, third, or even fourth language. As we'll discuss later in this book, multiple digital apps are also available that introduce children to diverse languages through developmentally appropriate, early literacy strategies by way of interactive games, stories, songs, and more.

According to the Multicultural Library Manifesto supported by the International Federation of Library Associations and Institutions (IFLA) and the United Nations Educational, Scientific, and Cultural Organization (UNESCO), "Each individual in our global society has the right to a full range of library and information services. In addressing cultural and linguistic diversity, libraries should:

◊ serve all members of the community without discrimination based on cultural and linguistic heritage;

◊ provide information in appropriate languages and scripts;

◊ give access to a broad range of materials and services reflecting all communities and needs;

◊ employ staff to reflect the diversity of the community, who are trained to work with and serve diverse communities." (IFLA and UNESCO 2012, par. 5)

To meet the precepts set forth by the manifesto, librarians striving to serve culturally diverse populations and promote cultural competence can engage in the following core actions:

◊ "develop culturally diverse and multilingual collections and services, including digital and multimedia resources;

◊ allocate resources for the preservation of cultural expression and heritage, paying particular attention to oral, indigenous and intangible cultural heritage;

◊ include programmes supporting user education, information literacy skills, newcomer resources, cultural heritage and cross-cultural dialogue as integral parts of the services;

◊ provide access to library resources in appropriate languages through information organization and access systems;

◊ develop marketing and outreach materials in appropriate media and languages to attract different groups to the library." (IFLA and UNESCO 2012, par. 11)

Using the information presented by the Multicultural Library Manifesto as a foundation for promoting cultural competence, children's librarians can provide opportunities for children and their families to interact with high-quality global children's literature in the first language of the family and can offer dynamic, culturally relevant literacy programs in the library throughout the calendar year. These programs can be used to connect all children with rich print and digital media representing their cultural experiences and to promote cultural competence by creating a forum for facilitating understanding and acceptance of diversity based on culture, ethnicity, linguistic ability, religion, physical ability, immigration status, sexual orientation, and other factors.

Examples of successful programs fostering cultural competence are highlighted in Chapter 5. However, an immediate example of using global literature to cultivate cultural competence can be seen in the historical work of Jella Lepman. Lepman created the International Youth Library (IYL) in Munich as a way to bridge the chasms in cultural understanding and knowledge left in Germany after World War II. See Figure 1.1 for a spotlight on her work. The next chapter describes how children's librarians can ensure successful programs that reflect many of the same goals as Lepman's work and can help children move beyond a single cultural story.

References

Abilock, Deborah, "Educating Students for Cross-Cultural Proficiency." *Knowledge Quest* 35, no. 2 (2006): 10–13.

Adichie, Chimamanda Ngozi. (October 2009). "The Danger of a Single Story." TEDtalk. Accessed February 14, 2014, at http://www.ted.com/talks/chimamanda_adichie_the_danger_of_a_single_story.html.

Bernbaum, Israel. "Forward." In *Mrs. Lepman: Give Us Books, Give Us Wings* edited by Lioba Betten (pp. 1-10). Munich: R. Kovar, 1992.

Cortés, Carlos. *The Making, and Remaking, of a Multiculturalist.* New York: Teachers College Press, 2002.

Geertz, Clifford. *The Interpretation of Cultures.* New York: Basic Books, 1973.

International Federation of Library Associations and Institutions (IFLA) and United Nations Educational, Scientific, and Cultural Organization (UNESCO). (2012). *Multicultural Library Manifesto.* Accessed February 24, 2014, at http://www.ifla.org/files/assets/library-services-to-multicultural-populations/publications/multicultural_library_manifesto-en.pdf.

Larson, Jeannette. (March 22, 2011). "Building a Culture of Literacy through Día: Library Events Celebrate Bilingual Bookjoy."

American Libraries. Accessed February 26, 2014, at: http://www.
    americanlibrariesmagazine.org/article/building-culture-literacy-
    through-d%C3%AD.

Metiri Group and North Central Regional Educational Laboratory
    (NCREL). "Profile of a Culturally Literate Student." Available at
    http://business.fullerton.edu/centers/CollegeAssessmentCenter/
    RubricDirectory/MulticultDiversity/MultiCulturalAwarenessRbrc.
    doc.

Montiel-Overall, Patricia. "Cultural Competence: A Conceptual
    Framework for Library and Information Science Professionals " *The
    Library Quarterly* 79, no. 2 (2009): 174–204.

Moreillon, Judi. "Building Bridges for Cultural Understanding: Cultural
    Literature Collection Development and Programming." *Children
    and Libraries* 11, no. 2 (2013): 35–38.

Nieto, Sonia. *The Light in Their Eyes: Creating Multicultural Learning
    Communities.* New York: Teachers College Press, 1999.

Ríos-Balderama, Sandra. "The Role of Cultural Competence in Creating a
    New Mainstream." *Colorado Libraries* 32, no. 4 (2006): 3–8.

Rosenblatt, Louise. *Literature as Exploration.* New York: The Modern
    Language Association of America, 1938.

Tanner, Karen, Alfreda Turner, Susan Greenwald, Chela Rios Munoz, and
    Sonia Ricks. "Cultural Sensitivity and Diversity Awareness: Bridging
    the Gap Between Families and Providers," *The Source* (AIA
    Resource Center) 6, no. 3 (1996): 1–3.

Tate, Binnie L. "The Role of the Children's Librarian in Serving the
    Disadvantaged." *Library Trends* 20 (October 1971): 392–404.

Vygotsky, L. (1978). *Mind and Society: The Development of Higher
    Psychological Processes.* Cambridge, MA: Harvard University Press.

Vygotsky, L. (1986). *Thought and Language.* Cambridge, MA: MIT Press.

Walter, Virginia A. *Twenty-First-Century Kids, Twenty-First-Century
    Librarians.* Chicago: ALA Editions, 2010.

Chapter 2

Criteria for Culturally Competent Programming

Providing library programs that support cultural competence can be one of the most rewarding jobs of a children's librarian. It can be heartwarming and motivating when an ordinarily shy child's face brightens because she makes a connection with a story or participates in an activity reminiscent of her home culture. As equally fulfilling is walking into your program room to discover it filled with families who have never visited the library before but decided to venture in because of the special cultural program that you've planned in the children's department.

Unfortunately, librarians can also become very frustrated with planning culture programs if they are met with roadblocks such as poorly attended programs, negative attitudes from colleagues or administration, or limited budgets that preclude the "pie in the sky" programs they want to plan. Too often, librarians interested in promoting cultural competence through library programming burn out or become frustrated before they start. Why? Creating cultural programs can be stressful, seemingly unappreciated, time consuming, and never-ending. Also, librarians who have never planned cultural programs may not know where to start. This chapter covers many important elements to consider when planning programs that promote cultural competence. Among the topics covered are how to plan programs that are not culturally offensive, how to get buy-in from important constituencies, where to find funding sources, where to find community partners, and how to assess a program's success.

Key Considerations for Developing Culturally Competent Services and Programs

When planning any type of program, librarians want to make the best use of their time and resources. It is important to schedule time well in advance to thoughtfully and carefully create a planning team, to reach out to the target audience, to secure space and funding, and to develop an evaluation plan. During the planning of culturally competent programming, librarians will want to consider the following:

◊ What are the demographics of the community served by your library and what are the informational, cultural, recreational, and educational needs? It is important for librarians to perform a community analysis and needs assessment. Part of this assessment includes discerning the strengths, weaknesses, opportunities, and threats involved in offering a particular library service to meet an identified community need.

◊ Who is the audience for your cultural programming? Remember that programs fostering cultural competence are for everyone, not just children and families from the cultural group being highlighted or celebrated.

◊ Is your library welcoming and inclusive to diverse cultural groups?

◊ Have you sought community input from local families about how to celebrate a particular cultural event and when the best time is to host the program?

◊ Are other comparable libraries serving similar culturally diverse populations? If so, what programs have been the most and least successful?

◊ Do you have a library collection that supports cultural programming? Will patrons find rich print and digital resources celebrating diversity and global cultures?

Library programs that promote cultural competence should not be singular or special events. To be effective and successful, children's librarians should incorporate cultural programs into their regular programming and align all their programs with the mission of the library. Most libraries have a mission statement that includes some variation of "expanding minds, empowering individuals, and enriching the community." With such a broad, inclusive statement, it is relatively easy for children's librarians to align their program goals with the library's mission. Essentially, the goals of most cultural programs are to link all children to print and digital materials in multiple languages about global cultures in order to expand minds and to empower and enrich communities.

In order for culturally competent programming to be successful, it cannot be considered a separate program for specialized populations, nor should it be marketed that way. For instance, when planning a program that includes a visit from an African American children's author such as Jacqueline Woodson, it would be a huge mistake to assume that only African American children and families will want to attend the program. While a librarian might want to target these children and families to ensure they know about the program, he or she will also want to promote and market the program throughout the entire community using a variety of online, digital, and traditional media outlets. Billing the program as an exciting event for all children and families to meet an award-winning author will bring in more people than advertising the program as an opportunity to meet a black author as part of Black History Month. If a program identifies in its promotional materials that it is focused on one specific culture, then children and families outside that culture may assume they are not welcome. However, if a librarian does want to highlight that a particular program is celebrating X culture, then promotional materials can emphasize the opportunity to learn about the rich heritage of culture X.

Even more successful and impactful would be to host year-round library programming about all types of cultures. Librarians who believe they must have targeted cultural programming should consider having a standard format repeated throughout the year for each targeted cultural program. This format should include opportunities for intercultural discussions and provide an avenue for community members from the spotlighted culture to share their experiences with other community members. This also creates a sense of ownership in the programming and helps to ensure community buy-in.

Develop Community Partnerships and Create Advisory Planning Committees

During the planning process for cultural programs, children's librarians will want to collaborate with local community organizations and enlist volunteers to make a small cultural celebration go far. With limited funding available in many libraries, community partnerships can mean the difference between having a successful event with a wide reach and having no program at all. Community partnerships can allow libraries to cost share expenses for authors, speakers, supplies, and so forth. Local organizations may have access to funding not readily available to libraries or may be able to provide in-kind donations of time, talents, supplies, food, and so on. Likewise, a partnership will allow the organization and the library to promote each other's services and programs, thereby broadening the reach to diverse segments of the community. This collaboration might also introduce librarians to the gatekeepers or important figures within a cultural community who can ensure participation in and success of a cultural program. Examples of potential community partners that have been fruitful to librarians include:

- Hospitals—particularly literacy-based programs such as Reach Out and Read
- Social services agencies
- Local businesses
- Ethnic and cultural associations—such as churches/synagogues, the Hispanic Interest Coalition of Alabama, the Greater Boston Chinese Cultural Association, the Western Pennsylvania Slovak Cultural Association, and the Gay and Lesbian Arab Society
- Museums and art centers
- Adult education centers
- Universities/schools/public libraries/educational institutions
- Civic organizations
- Literacy and advocacy organizations

The planning process for successful culturally competent programs will also include working with diverse cultural groups in the community to get community buy-in. While everyone should be invited to attend cultural celebrations and programs in the library, members of the cultural groups celebrated in a particular program should be included in the planning process. This is the secret to marketing and the ultimate success and impact of the program. In most cultural groups, there are notable individuals who are well respected within the community and serve in a gatekeeper capacity. By involving these key individuals in program planning, librarians can ensure that the program's content is culturally appropriate and responsive, that the timing of the program does not conflict with other major events within the cultural community, and that word about the program is successfully shared throughout the community. These community leaders often represent many diverse types of individuals such as successful businesspeople, educators, clergy, elders, and library volunteers. The buy-in of these gate-keepers can determine whether a program flourishes or not.

In some cases, these same community leaders are part of the library program advisory committee. This advisory committee, which includes members representative of community diversity, helps to ensure that cultural competence is modeled in children's library programs, collections, and services throughout the year. The advisory committee can serve in various roles that differ from library to library and can include the following tasks:

- Assisting librarians in the selection, acquisition, and use of culturally and linguistically diverse children's books
- Participating in the development of culturally responsive library programs that encourage children and families from all backgrounds to read for enjoyment and make cross-cultural connections
- Providing culturally responsive training and workshops for librarians, teachers, parents, and other adults to increase cultural competence about particular groups
- Helping to establish a community network of family and child services providers to share literacy practices and information regarding diverse communities in the local population
- Supporting librarians as they locate and examine best practices relating to library services and literacy programs for multicultural, multilingual populations

An example of how an advisory board can assist a librarian planning a cultural competence program looks something like the following:

> Altamont Public Library is situated within a community with a vastly growing Latino population. In the past, when the children's librarian attempted an outreach program celebrating Latino culture, it was poorly attended. Although fliers were printed in English and Spanish and distributed at the local Mexican restaurant, no Latino patrons attended the program. The children's librarian is frustrated; she knows Latino families are in the community but she does not know how to get them to come into the library. In desperation, she shares her disappointment with her library director, who suggests she consult the library's advisory board for ideas. Although there are no Latinos on the board, one of the members suggests the children's librarian contact local clergy where many Latinos attend church. After

consultation with the clergy, the librarian schedules a meeting with an active member of the congregation—a Latina mother of two elementary-aged children.

During this meeting, the children's librarian explains to the mother that she really wants to plan a library program that serves as a bridge of understanding to connect Latino and non-Latino families. She plans to include books and activities about Latino culture and hopes that Latino families will attend. The librarian also tells the mother about the previous unsuccessful program that she planned and wonders aloud why the program flopped. The mother explains that she never heard about the previous program but suggests the program may not have been success-ful because it was planned on a Saturday morning when many Latino parents are working. She recommends that she get a few other mothers together and meet with the librarian later.

Two weeks later, a buzz fills the library conference room where five very excited Latina mothers are brimming with ideas for a program that will feature famous Latino artists and musicians. Together, the librarian and mothers plan a bilingual Spanish-English program that includes games, songs, storytelling, read-alouds, hands-on art projects, and food. The librarian creates the English version of the flier and one of the mothers creates the Spanish version. Collectively, the librarian and the mothers pro-mote the program via print and digital media outlets. In addition, the mothers announce the program at the church. On the day of the program (at a date and time suggested by the mothers), the children's programming room has several extended families in attendance with approximately fifty children and tweens. Of these, about thirty are Latino. After the program is over the li-brarian meets with a few members of the library advisory board and the Latina mothers to evaluate the success of the program and debrief. Suggestions are provided for improvements such as ways to expand the program, community partners, and so forth, and plans are made for future programs that are inclusive of Latino culture but also celebrate other cultures.

In this scenario, the librarian was able to develop a rich relationship with a group of Latina mothers in the community through a series of events initiated by a recommendation of the library advisory board. While none of the members of the board represented the culture celebrated in the program, they provided suggestions for how the librarian could locate a gatekeeper in the community. Once the librarian worked with someone "on the inside," she understood why her other program was not successful and was able to plan a program that would be respectful and well attended. She also developed a relationship that will last beyond the one program and will lead to other successful programs. With the assistance of the advisory board and the mothers, the librarian was finally able to reach her target population and create a program that brought multiple cultures together.

Design Programs That Explore Diversity But Avoid Stereotypes

While a librarian may have good intentions to promote cultural competence in library programs, these plans are wasted if they inadvertently reinforce or teach cultural stereotypes. One of the easiest and most common ways for librarians and educators to introduce new cultures to children is through the Five Fs: food, fashion, festivals, famous people, and folklore. While this practice is not wholly objectionable, it cannot be the only way to explore global cultures. Children need opportunities for meaningful engagement with cultures that are different from their own. Librarians have to be very careful when using the Five Fs to avoid cultural stereotypes and tokenism. Often this approach tends to focus on cultural elements that are flashy, exotic, and quaint. Reading only folktales to children can give them a distorted view of a culture. Introducing them to unusual fashion or "costumes" and festivals from a culture that is different from their own can reinforce a sense of exoticism or otherness rather than fostering intercultural connections. Additionally, when librarians rely on the Five Fs to explore cultural diversity it is extremely problematic if any of the Fs are not culturally accurate or reinforce outdated stereotypes.

Good intentions are not good enough when librarians take a tourist approach to learning about cultures. In a tourist approach, librarians usually focus on the Five Fs and almost always relegate exploration of particular cultures to their "assigned" months: Black History Month, Hispanic Heritage Month, and so forth. The highest-quality materials and culturally authentic activities are irrelevant if children learn that their particular culture or the culture of their peers is not good enough to study or talk about throughout the year. While middle-class white children in heterosexual, nuclear families get to see their culture represented in the library and classroom on a daily basis, other children are lucky if they get their own special month or day!

A better way to explore diversity and build cultural competence is to provide meaningful opportunities for children to experience ways in which they are the "same, same but different" from children from other cultures. Demonstrating commonalities and then celebrating differences provides a lens that can help children develop cultural competence and make global connections. In her article "Classrooms Like Ours: Books About Schools Around the World," Patricia Stohr-Hunt highlights eighteen fiction and informational children's books that profile how children around the world receive their education. The topic of school is one that children can easily find relatable and provides the perfect opportunity for them to encounter a common experience through the lives of other global children. By exploring books such as those listed by Stohr-Hunt during a storytime, librarians can set the stage for rich learning experiences, particularly if the books are followed by hands-on activities that promote literacy and literary explorations into the various countries introduced. As we'll discuss later in this book, children's librarians can include digital media in the storytime, such as the *One Globe Kids* app or online library (http://oneglobekids.com/), where children are introduced to digital stories about the daily experiences of real children around the world.

Librarians unfamiliar with a particular culture may feel unqualified to plan programs representing its facets for fear that they will accidentally reinforce stereotypes or provide inaccurate information. Fortunately, numerous resources are available to assist librarians in choosing culturally appropriate literature and program activities to use in the children's library. These resources range from professional literature to library and literacy organizations to online recommended book and award lists. One of the best resources for helping librarians and educators understand the nuances in planning culturally sensitive lessons and programs that promote meaningful connections is *Beyond Heroes and Holidays: A Practical Guide to K–12 Anti-Racist, Multicultural Education and Staff Development* (Lee et al., 2008). This book provides considerable "food for thought" and provides different lenses for thinking about how cultural diversity is presented to children. Another timely resource for librarians filled with relevant information is the American Library Association's Programming Librarian website. This extensive Web resource provides librarians with program suggestions, links to grants, best practices articles, marketing information, learning opportunities, and more. While the general focus of the website is all types of library programming, one particular portion highlights multi-cultural programming to multiple age groups including children and families. See: http://www.programminglibrarian.org/tags.html?tags=multicultural+programming.

Various nonprofit organizations are dedicated to serving the information needs of specific cultural groups and provide useful toolkits, guidelines, and recommendations for building collections, creating services, and planning programs. A commonality among the goals and objectives of these organizations is a dedication to promoting high-quality services and programs that are reflective of and respectful to the people they represent. This includes representations in print and digital materials as well as ensuring that cultural programming is delivered respectfully and accurately. With all of this free information readily available from organizations such as those listed below, librarians can get a head start on planning the best children's programs promoting cultural competence.

- The American Indian Library Association is dedicated to serving the library needs of American Indians and Alaska Natives. http://www.ailanet.org/

- The Asian Pacific American Librarians Association (APALA) is committed to supporting librarians who serve Asian Pacific Americans. http://www.apalaweb.org/

- The Association for Specialized and Cooperative Library Agencies (ASCLA) helps librarians plan programs and services for differently-able individuals and incarcerated persons. http://www.ala.org/ascla/

- The Association of Jewish Libraries (AJL) promotes informational and cultural literacy about Jewish culture. http://www.jewishlibraries.org/main/

- The Black Caucus of the American Library Association (BCALA) is devoted to providing high-quality library services to African Americans. http://www.bcala.org/

- The Chinese American Librarians Association (CALA) aims to serve the informational needs of Chinese Americans. http://www.cala-web.org/

- The Ethnic and Multicultural Information Exchange Round Table (EMIERT) of the American Library Association is dedicated to assisting librarians serving various diverse populations including

African American, Armenian, and Jewish patrons. http://www.ala.
org/ala/mgrps/rts/emiert/index.cfm

◊ The Gay, Lesbian, Bisexual, and Transgender Round Table
(GLBTRT) of the American Library Association serves the literacy

Resources for Planning Library Programs Promoting Cultural Competence

◊ "Building Bridges for Cultural Understanding: Cultural Literature
Collection Development and Programming," (2013). Judi Moreillon.
Children and Libraries 11 (2): 35–38.

◊ "Cultural Diversity: How Public Libraries Can Serve the Diversity in
the Community." (2004). Jens Ingemann Larsen, Deborah L. Jacobs,
Ton van Vlimmeren. http://conferences.alia.org.au/alia2004/pdfs/
vlimmeren.t.paper.pdf

◊ "Implementing Family Literacy Programs for Linguistically and
Culturally Diverse Populations: Key Elements to Consider." (2004).
Delia C. Garcia and Deborah J. Hasson. *The School Community
Journal*. 14 (1): 113–137. http://eric.ed.gov/?id=EJ794831.

◊ *Library Services for Multicultural Patrons: Strategies to Encourage
Library Use*. Carol Smallwood and Kim Becnel (eds.). Jefferson, NC:
McFarland, 2013.

◊ *Library Youth Outreach: 26 Ways to Connect with Children, Young
Adults and Their Families*. Kerol Harrod and Carol Smallwood (eds.).
Jefferson, NC: McFarland, 2014.

◊ *Multicultural Storytime Magic*. Kathy MacMillan and Christine Kirker.
Chicago: American Library Association, 2012.

◊ "Multiculturalism Happens: Targeting Multicultural Literacy."
(2012). Gricel Dominguez. *Programming Librarian*. http://www.
programminglibrarian.org/library/planning/multiculturalism-happens-
targeting-multicultural-literacy-in-libraries.html#.Uwq-GvZsh3Y.

◊ *Travel the Globe: Story Times, Activities, and Crafts for Children*.
Desiree Webber, Dee Ann Corn, Elaine R. Harrod, Sandy Shropshire,
Shereen Rasor, and Donna Norvell. Santa Barbara, CA: Libraries
Unlimited, 2013.

Figure 2.1: Resources for Planning Library Programs Promoting Cultural Competence

and information needs of the GLBT library community, families, and other individuals. http://www.ala.org/glbtrt/glbtrt

◊ REFORMA or The National Association to Promote Library and Information Services to Latinos and the Spanish-Speaking is dedicated to assisting libraries with planning services and programs for Latinos. http://reforma.org/

For a list of other resources relating to planning culturally responsive programs for children see Figure 2.1. An extensive listing of professional resources and recommended online material is also available in the bibliography at the end of this book.

Program Evaluation and Funding

Two final points to consider when developing culturally competent programs for children and their families are program assessment and funding. Librarians put considerable time, energy, talent, and resources into planning programs that are culturally responsive. Sometimes this pays off with dynamic, engaging programs that are well-attended and widely featured in community media outlets. At other times, the programs are poorly attended or do not unfold as planned. Sometimes poorly attended programs can be hugely successful and heavily attended programs can be a disaster. How is a librarian to know if he or she is planning effective culturally competent programs?

The generally recognized practice for program evaluation that produces the most useful information and is often required by granting agencies is Outcomes Based Evaluation (sometimes referred to as Outcomes Based Planning and Evaluation). Outcomes are measureable changes in behavior, skill, attitude, knowledge, and so forth. This type of evaluation involves doing a needs assessment of the local community served by the library to determine the informational, recreational, and educational needs of specific cultural groups, developing program goals based on these identified needs, and then measuring to see how well these goals or outcomes are met. Outcomes Based Evaluation (OBE) is accomplished via observations, interviews, focus groups, surveys, and so on, providing both quantitative and qualitative information that can be used to determine a program's success. According to Anderson (2014), "if you start your program planning by connecting with the people you're serving or want to serve (or at least with other people working with them), you are more likely to: develop programming that is really meaningful and attractive to them; schedule and locate your programs effectively (and possibly include a transportation component) because you know more about their schedules, obligations, and habits; and connect more effectively with the right people with your marketing, and benefit more powerfully from word-of-mouth (always the best PR)." (par. 3)

Rubin (2004) observes that OBE is one of the most effective forms of library evaluation. The value of OBE is that it:

◊ Clarifies the purpose of the program/service
◊ Keeps staff and stakeholders focused on goals by stressing "so what" rather than process
◊ Stimulates discussion of issues
◊ Helps keep implementation on track; milestones are identified
◊ Indicates when changes to a program are needed
◊ Energizes library staff by demonstrating the real, human impact their work produces and by stressing common purposes and goals
◊ Gives insight into why and how library services are used; new perspective on library services in context of the user
◊ Assists in fundraising and grant writing by providing statistics on results
◊ Provides empirical evidence that what you are doing is what you intended to do
◊ Quantifies the anecdotes and success stories
◊ Identifies effective programs/services
◊ Demonstrates the library's contribution to solving community problems
◊ Demonstrates accountability as required by IMLS [the Institute of Museum and Library Services] (Rubin 2004)

For information on how to create program evaluation questions and tools, consult the Association for College and Research Libraries' Tips for Program Evaluation Forms (available at http://www.ala.org/acrl/aboutacrl/directoryofleadership/sections/is/iswebsite/about/resources/tipsprogrameval) as well as the Program Evaluation section of the Programming Librarian initiative (http://www.programminglibrarian.org/library/planning/program-evaluation.html#.Uww0evZsh3Y).

Funding for cultural programming is essential for program success. While a fantastic program does not have to cost a fortune to implement, a reliable funding source can make planning much simpler and allow a children's librarian to bring in speakers or authors, purchase food and supplies for program activities, or acquire books and equipment to be used during a particular program. In an age when many library budgets are tight, library programming—particularly cultural programming—can be one of the first areas cut. As such, it is important for librarians committed to planning culturally competent programming to know where to find dedicated funding sources by way of grants. The following grants are designed specifically for children's cultural programming.

- Light the Way Grant: Outreach to the Underserved Grant (http://www.ala.org/alsc/awardsgrants/profawards/ candlewicklighttheway)—Awarded by the Association for Library Service to Children and sponsored by Candlewick Press, this grant supports an exemplary library outreach program for underserved children. According to the grant website, "Special population children may include those who have learning or physical differences, those who speak English as a second language, those who are in a non-traditional school environment, those who live in foster care settings, those who are in the juvenile justice system, those who live in gay and lesbian families, those who have teen parents, and those who need accommodation service to meet their needs."

- Ezra Jack Keats Minigrant Program for Public Libraries and Public Schools (http://www.ezra-jack-keats.org/minigrant-program/)— Awarded by the Ezra Jack Keats Foundation, these grants fund activities that "foster creative expression, working together and interaction with a diverse community." Cultural programs funded in the past have included pen-pal projects bringing disparate communities together; multicultural portrait projects; art projects culminating in art shows, murals, or quilts; creation of puppet shows or plays; bookmaking; and intergenerational journals.

- Estela and Raul Mora Award (http://www.reforma.org/mora_ award)—Awarded by REFORMA (the National Association to Promote Library and Information Services to Latinos and the Spanish-Speaking) and sponsored by Latina children's author and poet Pat Mora and her siblings, this award/grant retroactively funds an exemplary cultural literacy program that celebrates Día: Children's Day, Book Day.

◊ Día Family Book Club Grants (http://dia.ala.org/)—Awarded by the Association for Library Service to Children and funded by Dollar General Literacy Foundation, these grants fund library programs that host book clubs, book discussion groups, and book-themed activities that promote cultural understanding and intercultural connections.

◊ Talk Story: Sharing Stories, Sharing Culture Grants (http://talkstorytogether.org/grants)—Awarded by the American Indian Library Association and the Asian Pacific American Librarians Association and funded by Toyota Financial Services, these grants fund programs that "celebrate and explore Asian Pacific American (APA) and American Indian/Alaska Native (AIAN) stories through books, oral traditions, and art to provide an interactive, enriching experience."

In addition to the grants listed above, librarians may find other grants dedicated to developing collections, services, or programs for specific multicultural populations. For instance, the Alabama Public Library Service provides Library Services and Technology Act (LSTA) grants from IMLS that fund a variety of library activities. Usually there is a category each year relating to programs or collections for multicultural or underserved populations.

Concluding Thoughts

In this chapter we have discussed many important elements to consider when planning culturally competent library programs for children and families. While we have not provided an exhaustive list of considerations, the information should provide a foundation for starting the journey of planning children's programs that promote cultural competence. The resources listed here and at the end of the book supply additional, detailed information on the specific nuances of planning these types of programs and highlight examples of recommended materials and specialized cultural programs for children.

This chapter also lays the groundwork for planning cultural programs that incorporate the use of digital media. The following chapters build on this foundation, providing rationales for including digital media in the children's library as well as evaluation criteria for selecting high-quality, culturally responsive digital apps, e-books, and more.

References

Anderson, Abbie. "Meeting Needs and Making a Difference: Outcomes Based Planning and Evaluation." *Programming Librarian.* Accessed February 24, 2014, at http://www.programminglibrarian.org/library/planning/meeting-needs.html#.Uwwq7_Zsh3Y.

Lee, Enid, Deborah Menkart, and Margo Okazawa-Rey. *Beyond Heroes and Holidays: A Practical Guide to K-12 Anti-Racist, Multicultural Education and Staff Development.* 4th ed. Washington, D.C.: Teaching for Change, 2008.

Rubin, Rhea Joyce. (2004). "So What? Using Outcome-Based Evaluation to Assess the Impact of Library Services." Accessed February 25, 2014, at http://mblc.state.ma.us/grants/lsta/manage/obe/rubinobemanual.doc.

Stohr-Hunt, Patricia. "Classrooms like Ours: Books About Schools Around the World." *Book Links*, 20 no. 1 (2011): 15–18.

II

Digital Media, Children, and the Library

Chapter 3

Digital Media in the Lives of Children

The children's department is often the first place outside the home that a young person feels a sense of belonging. Youth librarians deserve a lot of credit for making the library one of the warmest, most welcoming environments a child can experience. Technology doesn't have to be in opposition to this. Rather, it's an opportunity for librarians to show how digital and analog skills can blend together using the same level of humanity that occurs at storytime. It's a chance to start teaching digital literacy skills at an early age, and help parents and caregivers to recognize that technology can be something more than just an electronic babysitter (Greenwalt, 2013, p. 18).

This chapter explores many concepts such as transmedia and multiliteracies of 21st-century children and the role of libraries in promoting these literacies. We also discuss the role of digital media in the lives and development of children and examine how new digital media can be used in libraries and other educational settings. The information covered captures the essence of the quote at the beginning of this chapter and helps to lay the foundation for how and why librarians should consider using digital media in their children's programs.

The Role of Libraries in Literacy Development

Fostering a culture of literacy is a key function of libraries around the world. Whether providing opportunities to explore traditional reading literacy, practice Web literacy skills, develop higher-order thinking skills, promote cultural literacy, spark artistic and creative energies, facilitate digital literacy, or scaffold life-long learning, public libraries have the potential to be the heart of their communities, creating a "third space" (informal public gathering space) where children and families, teenagers, and adults of all ages can come together. According to a recent study examining the impact of public libraries, 95 percent of Americans ages 16 and older affirm that the public library is integral in promoting literacy and a love of reading in the community (Pew Research Center, 2013). The Institute of Museum and Library Services' (2013) report *Growing Young Minds: How Museums and Libraries Create Lifelong Learners* emphasizes the role of the library in promoting multiliteracies and in closing the achievement gap between low-income and high-income children. The report describes ten major ways in which museums and libraries support early literacy skills, STEM learning, Common Core Standards, digital literacy, and more to help children in the community succeed in educational attainment and growth. Of particular significance to our discussion of why the library should incorporate digital media in the library is number seven on the list: the ability of museums and libraries to link new digital technology to learning. According to the report, "With their free public access to the Internet, libraries are important community digital hubs, with expertise in promoting digital, media, and information literacy. Museums and school and public libraries are rich sources of accessible digital media, educational apps, videos, and audio- and e-books, with staff trained to help parents and youth select age-appropriate, content-based, curriculum-linked materials. They help close the digital divide for children, families, and caregivers who lack alternate sources of access" (IMLS 2013, p. 22). That is, libraries *should* provide access to digital media including educational apps, e-books, etc., and we *should* promote digital, media, and information literacy. Most librarians understand their role in promoting traditional reading and information literacy, but some are not so certain they should be promoting digital or media literacy. Does promoting digital or media literacy take away from the library's goal to promote the love of reading and books?

Multiliteracies extend beyond traditional notions of literacy (reading and writing) to include information, web, media, digital, cultural, and other literacies needed for digital natives—children born since the saturation of the Internet, digital media, and other technologies into their daily home and school lives—to function in today's wired and culturally pluralistic society. Children may employ one or all of these literacies in various capacities at any point during the day. Children often use more than one of these literacies at a time and it can be difficult to separate them. For the purposes of this book, we will address each type of literacy individually. Web literacy differs from information literacy in that information literacy concerns being able to locate and evaluate information while Web literacy involves knowing how to use the various tools (hardware and software) for information retrieval and exchange. Information literacy is a higher-order skill that requires the ability to think critically; Web literacy requires working knowledge of how Internet resources function. Mastery of Web literacy is required before successfully exhibiting information literacy. Children need to know how to use or navigate a wiki, blog, website, or other Internet resource before they can evaluate and use the information within it.

Along with information and web literacies goes the concept of media literacy. Media literacy relates to a child's ability to evaluate the social messages expressed in a particular piece of media: movie, video game, book, newspaper, advertisement, app, website, and so forth. Children interact with media on a daily basis and should understand that every media source has an underlying objective—to inform, persuade, inculcate, sell a product, and so on. Children who are media literate can identify the message being communicated and discern how it applies to their lives and environment. Sometimes the concept of visual literacy is presented as a component of media literacy and other times it is treated separately. Visual literacy is the ability to understand visual cues, signs, and other elements as well as the placement of various elements within illustrations, pictures, photographs, and other images. All images carry a message that contributes to the social message in a particular piece of media. When a child looks at the illustrations in a book or interacts with visual images in a digital app, he or she is presented with cues, signs, and symbols meant to represent a particular concept or message. Librarians and other educators are charged with helping children understand what these images are saying and how this makes the child feel about a particular topic, cultural group, or other aspect. If stereotypical images are portrayed, then children need help understanding why the images are wrong and the negative influences these images can have on the viewer.

The idea of digital literacy combines elements of web, information, media, and visual literacies and describes the ability of children to consume, communicate, and create with digital media. As librarians and educators it is our responsibility to help children become responsible digital citizens who understand that the information they create and distribute using digital media is shared worldwide and never really disappears from the virtual world. Children should be responsible digital citizens and not create or share digital media that is physically harmful or emotionally hurtful to other people.

Cultural literacy or multicultural literacy is the term used to describe an understanding and respect for diverse cultures. For a child to function successfully in a culturally pluralistic society, he or she must understand that everyone's culture is unique and know how to engage positively with a diverse group of people. Cultural literacy is an underlying component of other literacies. Children who are culturally literate can identify negative depictions of their culture and that of others in the social messages in the text and images of various types of print and digital media. In Chapter 1, we looked at the idea of cultural competence. Children must first exhibit cultural literacy before they can become culturally competent. Some sociologists and educators suggest that we never fully reach cultural competence; rather, it is something we strive toward throughout our lives. Nonetheless, cultural literacy is the first step toward cultural competency. Library programs that foster cultural literacy can help children and families begin this journey.

Why is it important to understand the various types of literacies? Whenever children are in the library reading books, interacting with digital apps, playing online games, or searching for answers to homework, they are employing one or more of the aforementioned literacies. As children's librarians it is our role to facilitate literacy development in all its formats. It is important to keep in mind that multiliteracies underlie the activities and media we select when planning children's library programs.

Transmedia

As we continue our journey to better understanding the role of media and various literacies in the lives of contemporary digital natives, the next logical destination is a discussion of transmedia or the interplay between and among various types of print and digital media to discover new information and to use new digital media to express creativity and learning. According to researchers at University of Southern California's Annenberg Innovation Lab and the Joan Ganz Cooney Center at Sesame Workshop, transmedia play has exciting potential for meeting the diverse learning needs of digital natives: "Through immersive, interconnected, and dynamic narratives, transmedia engages multiple literacies, including textual, visual, and media literacies, as well as multiple intelligences. It is highly engaging and allows for important social sharing among collaborators" (Herr-Stephenson et al., 2013, p. 12). These researchers further suggest that transmedia play and storytelling

◊ promote reading approaches that combine navigation and interplay between print and digital books

◊ encourage learning through joint media engagement among children and between children and their families

◊ support a constructivist model of learning that empowers children to create knowledge from their contextual surroundings and drive their learning experiences (Herr-Stephenson et al., 2013, p. 2).

Of particular interest to librarians is transmedia's potential to extend learning between print and digital children's books. Jenkins (2013) emphasizes, "Transmedia encourages additive comprehension. We learn something new as we follow the story across media. This distinguishes it from cross-media, which refers to the use of these other media platforms as simple delivery mechanisms for the same old content" (p. 7). A successful children's library program will incorporate both print and digital media to create an interactive environment that extends learning and comprehension. If a librarian chooses to read a Curious George book during a story program and then follows with a purposefully chosen, highly engaging and interactive digital app featuring Curious George, then children can begin making connections between the two media, particularly when the digital app is first shared with the entire group on an overhead screen and then children are allowed to explore the app themselves on individual digital tablets. To further the concept of transmedia, librarians can follow the story reading and digital play with a hands-on activity where children create a retelling or extension of the Curious George story through reader's theatre or using puppets. This retelling could be recorded and posted on the library's YouTube channel. Alternatively, children could create a comic strip or sock puppet play using digital apps and present their comic strips or sock puppet plays to the other children and families attending the library program. "Good transmedia experiences scaffold children's participation—supporting them through tasks such as asking and answering questions, making connections between information, creating media, and sharing creations with others. Such activities, in and of themselves, are examples of constructivist learning" (Herr-Stephenson et al., 2013, p. 23).

This last statement is very important for librarians to remember because they may face opposition to transmedia and the inclusion of new digital media in children's library programs. Sometimes fellow librarians, library supervisors, and caregivers are resistant to the inclusion of new digital media in the traditional children's storytime. For many, there is a fear that the digital media will overpower or overshadow the books. When used correctly and thoughtfully and in the spirit of transmedia play and storytelling, the inclusion of new digital media in children's library programs can empower children to create learning experiences that meet their individualized learning style and engage multiple intelligences. Librarian Jennifer Hopwood (2013) emphasizes that using transmedia storytelling in the library can be a great way to reach boys and reluctant readers as it "provides many outlets back to reading; there are books based on video game characters, cartoons, movies, etc. Things are kept interesting because they are extensions of the originals, not just retellings in a different format" (par. 6). Children who may not ordinarily be interested in reading may have a spark ignited through transmedia storytelling.

Allow a personal anecdote to highlight this point. As a former school and children's librarian and current library educator, I am often hesitant and a little embarrassed to admit that my love of reading was not sparked by a passionate librarian or a piece of high-quality children's literature. Indeed, my passion for reading engagement was sparked by an "old school" form of transmedia offered in the late 1970s and early 1980s—licensed children's books representing toys and cartoon characters. It was not Corduroy, Babar, Madeline, or a series of ducklings "to make way for" that grabbed my attention as a young boy. Rather, it was Smurfs, Care Bears, Muppets, Disney's Alice in Wonderland, and the toy version of Raggedy Ann and Andy that fed my desire to read. I would watch the cartoons or holiday specials with these characters and then seek out books to further explore the adventures of my favorite character. I would then use ViewMaster reels to get a different media experience before going back to the children's programs and books. Records and later cassette tapes allowed me to further explore the lives of my friends and inspired me to create my own retellings of stories involving these characters. Sometimes these stories were written out and other times they were acted out with my toys. While I eventually graduated to more "quality" and "classic" children's literature, seeking out Carroll's *Alice's Adventures in Wonderland,* Gruelle's *Raggedy Ann Stories* and *Raggedy Andy Stories,* and Peyo's original comic books involving the Smurfs along the way, it was the transmedia experiences with these licensed characters that fueled my continued interest in reading. Later when I became a librarian myself, I disagreed with colleagues who saw licensed children's materials as the scourge of children's literature. My belief, one that I know other librarians supportive of transmedia storytelling endorse, is that *if* you can hook a reluctant child with a licensed product and get him or her passionate about reading and *if* you can provide meaningful and interactive learning experiences that build upon each other, *then* you can eventually introduce the child to other "quality" materials. Librarians need to grab reluctant readers' attention first with transmedia storytelling or other types of digital media.

Later in this chapter we will discuss why some researchers, teachers, librarians, and caregivers are hesitant to use new digital media with children, particularly young children. First, however, we would like to explore some of the various types of new digital media that can be used with children and their families in the library.

Types of New Digital Media

When thinking about how to use new digital media in library programs, it is essential to understand the unique learning opportunities that various types of new digital media offer children and their families. A non-interactive digital picture book or e-book for children is quite different from an interactive website or digital app that encourages children to tap, swipe, and explore a particular topic or story. Although this book admittedly focuses heavily on digital picture book/storybook apps for tablets, it also covers other types of digital media such as subscription-based and free digital picture books, e-books, and creative and gaming websites. Downloadable audiobooks for children, such as those found on OverDrive, and book trailers are considered relatively new digital media for children, but they only receive a passing mention from time to time.

Non-Interactive or Limited Interaction E-Books

E-books are static digital documents, usually in a PDF or Epub format. For the most part, e-books are created for specialized e-readers (such as Nooks or Kindles) and have limited interactivity options beyond resizing text, highlighting particular passages, searching content for specific words or phrases, and audio narration. Some e-books for children are predominantly text based, such as digital version of a children's novel, and other e-books include photographs and illustrations that would be found in the print version of a children's picture book. E-books are usually scans of the print version of a particular title. Like all materials for children, the quality of e-books differs greatly. Because their interactivity is quite limited, the potential for using e-books in children's library programming is primar-

Radical Change, Multiliteracies, and Interactive Picture Books

In 1999 library and information science professor Eliza Dresang published her seminal *Radical Change: Books for Youth in a Digital Age,* which describes how children's literature is changing to embrace multiliteracies and provide multiple layers of meaning (multimodal texts). She also explains that changes in the format of print books are directly related to creating texts that hold characteristics of online content in webpages such as sidebars, chunked information, and so forth. In essence, the boundaries between printed and digital media begin to blur. Books such as *Lucky Monkey/Unlucky Monkey* (Kaczman, 2008) included interruptions in the linear narrative via animals with speech bubbles. Readers can either ignore the animals' commentary or diverge to discover what the animals have to say. This resembles the pop-up windows and messages that children encounter when they use various websites. By introducing this nonlinear reading via a printed children's book, librarians can scaffold the children's thinking about how to navigate online resources with nonlinear text.

As technology has changed, print picture books have been published that foster the use of multiliteracies needed to navigate and interact with children's apps. Two recent titles for young children that fit this description are *Press Here* (Tullet, 2011) and *Tap the Magic Tree* (Matheson, 2013). In both books, the reader is asked to perform a motion (press, tap, blow, swipe, shake, etc.) involving the page or entire book. Once the motion is performed, readers turn the page to see what has happened as a result of their interaction. The similarities to interactive storybook apps are uncanny, particularly in the case of Matheson's book. Children learn about the cause and effect of their actions and gain skills that will help them navigate digital apps. Librarians and educators who want to foster the development of digital literacy skills can use these books to introduce young children and their parents to motions necessary to interact with an app on digital tablets. This would be particularly effective as a precursor to a library program incorporating tablets. At the same time, these books also help librarians address

ily confined to displaying the books on the overhead to read as a group during storytime or making them available on computers and other digital devices in the children's area for independent perusal. This is not to say that e-books do not have a place in the children's library. On the contrary, the International Children's Digital Library (http://www.childrenslibrary.org/)

various Common Core Standards for children in primary grades and promote STEM learning. Cross-curricular activities than can be used with *Tap the Magic Tree* are available from HarperCollins (http://www.thepageturn.com/blog/wp-content/uploads/2013/08/Tap-the-Magic-Tree-TG-FINAL.pdf).

3-D printers are also being used in the children's library to provide rich learning experiences for today's digital natives. These printers can be used in makerspaces as part of passive programming or in structured children's programs. The children's picture book *LEO The Maker Prince* (Diana, 2013) is the first book that allows children to print out the characters with a 3-D printer to use for creative play. Imagine the possibilities of children using this technology and

Tap the Magic Tree by Christie Matheson. Greenwillow/Harper, 2013.

multiliteracies to explore global literature and cultures from around the world. Rather than simply reading about culture and interacting with the characters through traditional methods of reader response, children can experience the culture and engage with characters through physical objects represented in the illustrations or text. More information about 3-D printers in children's libraries is available from the Webjunction article "3D-Printers: A Revolution Headed for Your Library" (http://www.webjunction.org/news/webjunction/3D_Printer_Revolution.html) and Make It @ Your Library (http://makeitatyourlibrary.org/), an extensive website with information on successful strategies for makerspaces, created in collaboration with Instructables.com and the American Library Association.

Figure 3.1: Radical Change, Multiliteracies, and Interactive Picture Books

provides an extensive, free online global collection of e-books in a variety of languages. This resource is invaluable to children's librarians, teachers, and other educators who may need titles in a particular language but do not have the budget to order them or who need them immediately. For instance, if you have a family move into your community that is fluent in Serbian and you do not have a current collection of Serbian children's materials, then the International Children's Digital Library can provide immediate access to non-interactive e-books in Serbian. Resources such as this allow a librarian to extend the existing collection to include hard-to-find or out-of-print titles and to meet the literacy needs of limited-English-proficient children and families.

Interactive Digital Picture Books

Interactive digital picture books are becoming more and more popular. "Interactivity can relate to both 'navigation' through the digital text and story construction. Navigation concerns the selection of participation options such as having the story read to you or reading it yourself, and in the latter case then determining how to change to the next screen . . . knowing how to 'quit' the story and return to it, and whether returning necessitates starting from the beginning or whether you can go directly to a particular page somewhere in the story" (Unsworth et al., 2005, p. 23). The International Children's Digital Library includes digital picture books (scans of the original printed picture book) but they are not interactive. True interactive digital picture books allow for the navigation described by Unsworth and are the precursor to digital storybook or picture-book apps. Often interactive digital picture books will include animations, sounds, music, and expressive readings of the text. As with other forms of digital media, interactive digital picture books include both free and fee-based options (often in the form of a subscription). Usually these books run directly from an online website and don't reside on your local hardware devices. Many libraries make these available to patrons on the library's children's department webpage, and librarians will use them in storytimes to supplement print stories or extend learning on a particular topic. Recently, storybook apps (such as those from TumbleBook and One More Story) featuring these interactive digital picture books have appeared for tablets and other mobile devices. In some cases modifications have been made to include more interactivity, and in other cases the digital picture book is the same but it is shared on the tablet app rather than via a website.

Recommended Free and Subscription-Based Interactive Digital Picture Books

Between the Lions—Free digital children's books with audio, music, and animated illustrations. Books are divided according to genre. http://pbskids.org/lions/stories/.

Capstone Interactive Library—Subscription digital books featuring nonfiction, graphic novels, and more. Includes narration and music. http://www.mycapstonelibrary.com/index.html.

One More Story—Subscription digital storybooks. Libraries can sign up for a free trial and view the books. Includes animations, highlighting of words as they are being read, music, and audio. http://onemorestory.com/.

Scholastic BookFlix—Subscription digital storybooks. Combines Weston Woods storybook videos with nonfiction digital picture books. Includes animations, sound, and reading of the text. http://teacher.scholastic.com/products/bookflixfreetrial/index.htm.

Starfall—Contains various free interactive early literacy games, original books, etc., for young children. Letters are sounded out for beginning readers and some of the books are levelized by reading ability. http://www.starfall.com/.

Storyline Online—Free digital storybooks read by famous stars from the Actors Guild. Includes audio and video of the actor reading the story and occasional static illustrations from the book. http://www.storylineonline.net/.

Toon Books—An imprint of Candlewick Press. These digital graphic novels for young children are levelized and available for free in a variety of languages. Some include narration and sound. http://www.toon-books.com/toon-online-readers.html.

Tumblebooks—Subscription digital storybooks. Uses some animation such as turning pages, blinking eyes, small movements, etc. As the book is read aloud, the words are highlighted to help beginning readers with word recognition. http://www.tumblebooks.com/.

Figure 3.2: Recommended Free and Subscription-Based Interactive Digital Picture Books

For a list of common, reputable free and subscription interactive digital picture books see Figure 3.2.

Creative and Gaming Websites

Interactive creative and gaming websites are another form of digital media that has potential for use in children's programs. With these websites, children can explore a particular concept or topic via creative online craft activities, educational games, virtual songbooks, and more! Libraries can bookmark particular websites for passive programming on children's library computers or to be used while children wait turns for hands-on craft activities during a storytime program. Some of the educational and creative apps available for children began on creative and gaming websites. Interactive websites provide opportunities for transmedia play by providing alternative platforms to printed books and digital apps to explore characters and stories. An example of a creative website for children is the New York Philharmonic's Kid Zone (http://www.nyphilkids.org/main.phtml?), which allows children to make their own instruments and compose their own music. The Association for Library Service to Children (ALSC) provides a comprehensive and growing list of notable websites for children on their Great Websites for Kids (http://gws.ala.org/). Many of these websites include creative and gaming activities. Examples of creative and gaming websites with multicultural content will be explored later in Chapter 7.

Apps

Apps are stand-alone software applications—generally created for the Android or Apple operating systems—that run on a mobile digital device such as a smartphone or digital tablet. They can be free or purchased for a nominal fee. When a new app is developed it may be offered for free and then later made available for purchase. Sometimes both free and fee versions of an app are available, with the fee version offering more features, tools, and so forth. Depending on the creator of the app, they can be passive, where the children have very little interaction, or interactive, where children drive the action through various cause-and-effect motions (tapping, swiping, etc.). According to Jennifer Gal (2013), two types of apps exist: native and adaptive. Native apps were originally created for the digital tablet and the interactivity seems more organic. Adaptive apps were originally in another format—an online game, a printed book, static e-book, for example—and have been adapted to the tablet software. Sometimes functionality and interactivity on adaptive apps can seem "off," creating problems or frustrations for the user.

Children's apps are divided into three major categories: book apps, gaming apps, and creative apps. Book apps include storybook/picture book apps and e-book apps. The interactivity within the app varies greatly from product to product, but the best type of book app for the children's library is an interactive storybook app designed to engage children and extend learning concepts via developmentally appropriate screen interactions. Interactive storybook apps usually have sound (narration, music, etc.), internal games, and hotspots where a child points to something on the screen to cause an action, narration, and sometimes animation. Guernsey and Levine (2012) observe that "Good e-books [storybook apps] for building strong readers will ask questions that lead to interactions with on-screen images that add meaning to the story or help reinforce the storyline. Ideally, such e-books, coupled with parenting programs in early childhood programs and libraries, could help parents see their value in helping their children, especially for moms and dads who have never felt all that confident reading aloud print books" (par. 6). For a fascinating look at the evolution of storybook apps, consult Sarah Towle's webcast "A Brief History of StoryApps and Interactivity" (http://www.youtube.com/watch?v=z_1Elo6-Qfs).

Gaming apps consist of a series of challenges and levels to be achieved via some type of digital strategy game. Some gaming apps, called educational apps/educational gaming apps, are created for the specific purpose of teaching a skill or concept. Other gaming apps mirror typical video and computer games and are created for entertainment purposes. Activities might unintentionally teach a skill or concept and there may be violence such as kicking, punching, and killing. The best gaming apps for libraries are those that are developmentally appropriate for children and are created to teach a skill or concept in a fun, engaging, and interactive fashion.

Creative apps provide specific tools, activities, and opportunities to develop or design an end product such as a digital story, puppet show, or felt board scene. Like all other apps, these range in quality and age-appropriateness for children depending on the designer. The best creative apps are non-prescriptive, allow for free play, and promote educational exploration and engagement. Sometimes the most successful use of creative apps is to profile them during a storytime and then allow children free play via individual tablets or tablet kiosks.

Keep in mind that this is a very high-level overview of digital media for children. Multiple other forms of digital media exist; this chapter has only discussed a few that can be used in the children's library. Additional examples of digital media will be discussed in Chapter 7 when we examine materials that can be used in library programs to promote cultural competence among children, their peers, and their families. In the subsequent section we will examine the ongoing discussion regarding the use of digital media with children and the potential effects.

Digital Media and Child Development

Over the past few decades, numerous reports from researchers, child psychologists, and pediatricians have suggested that screen time for young children should be significantly limited or entirely eradicated. The Committee on Public Education of the American Academy of Pediatrics report (1999), updated in 2011, is an example of the earliest of these warnings about screen time. (For a detailed overview of these studies see Guernsey [2012]). Almost all of these red-flag reports indicate that screen time—TV viewing, computer and mobile device usage, etc.—can be detrimental to a child's cognitive and emotional development, particularly if the screen time includes passive viewing and involves children under the age of two. Experts, researchers, librarians, teachers, and other educators seem to cover a wide spectrum of opinions on the issue of screen time (which includes technology use) with children, particularly young children. In 1996 the National Association for the Education of Young Children (NAEYC) published an initial statement about the use of technology with children ages three to eight, officially supporting technology integration in learning programs for young children. Recently NAEYC partnered with the Fred Rogers Center for Early Learning and Children's Media (2012) to revise the 1996 statement to include new digital media and to address concerns about technology and digital media usage with infants and young children. This statement suggests how *developmentally appropriate* technology in its multiple formats can be purposefully integrated into learning environments. The term *developmentally appropriate* is key to positive, educational learning experiences for children. There are many types of print and digital media available for children; and just as books or films are created for a specific age range, new digital media are also developed for assigned age ranges based on physical and psychological developmental stages. Apps that are appropriate for an eight-year-old child will not be engaging for a two-year-old.

The premise of the position statement of the NAEYC and the Fred Rogers Center was echoed twenty years ago by children's literature scholar

Margaret Mackey, who observed the importance of connecting new media with children's literature, stating "to talk about children's literature, in the normal restricted sense of children's novels, poems and picture-books, is to ignore the multi-media expertise of our children" (1994, p. 17). Certainly, the majority of digital natives in classrooms and libraries today have more "multi-media expertise" than their counterparts in the mid-1990s. To ignore the significance of new digital media in the lives of children and the potential for enriched cross-cultural literary experiences discounts the changing forms of literacy in our society.

According to Lisa Guernsey (2012), noted expert on the use of new media with children, it is okay and even encouraged for young children to interact with digital media as long as educators, librarians, and caregivers consider the following: content, context, and the individual child. First, what are the messages and purposes conveyed via a particular digital media. Are children learning a new skill? Are the activities developmentally appropriate? To this we would add: what social messages about particular cultural groups do children take away from a particular digital app, digital picture book, e-book, etc. Are stereotypes being created or reinforced?

The context of how a particular digital media is used with a child is also important. Is it serving as a distraction for the child so the caregiver or educator can do other things? Is the experience meant to be educational or entertaining? Are children actively engaged with the digital media or only passive bystanders? How long is a child in front of the screen? Is the child alone or with other children or adults? Another consideration when using digital media with young children is to understand that each child develops differently, uniquely, and what may work for one child or group of children may not be successful or relevant for other children. While one child may flourish with a diet of equal parts social interaction with peers, screen time, and engagement with print, another child may need a greater dose of one or the other depending on his/her individual physical and cognitive development.

One important element to remember is that children need social interaction and physical contact with other children, caregivers, teachers, librarians, and other educators. Digital media interaction should not always be a solo activity. Rather, children should be engaged in joint media engagement with their peers, caregivers, librarians, teachers, and others. The digital literacy skills of caregivers and educators also play a pivotal role in the level and extent of joint media engagement. If the adults in a child's life are not knowledgeable about how to use digital media technologies, their level of engagement with the child will be hindered. Socioeconomic status also plays a role in the level of joint media engagement. If caregivers do not have access to digital media, their level of digital literacy will be lower than that of caregivers who have ready access to digital media. The digital divide between those with access to technology/digital media and those without creates an environment where low-income caregivers are not as actively engaged in joint media engagement as their higher-income peers. During a two-year study in two vastly different public libraries in the Philadelphia area, Neuman and Celano (2012) observed that caregivers from more economically disadvantaged areas did not actively engage with their children during technology use whereas high-income caregivers did. Similarly, the higher-income caregivers provided opportunities for children to experience higher-order thinking and reasoning skills while the lower-income caregivers did not.

These findings are significant for librarians who are considering the use of digital media in children's programming. Based on classic reports such as *Becoming a Nation of Readers* (Anderson et al., 1985), librarians understand the importance of reading aloud to all children from the time they are born. It is understood that children from low-income areas often do not receive the same early literacy experiences as their high-income counterparts and will start school at a disadvantage. Hence, the creation of Every Child Ready to Read and other early literacy initiatives promoted by the American Library Association to help close the literacy gap between low-income children and their higher socioeconomic peers. This reasoning can also be applied to help young children and their parents develop digital literacy skills in the library. By selecting and using interactive digital media in storytimes that scaffold joint media engagement and higher-order thinking, librarians can help lower-income children and parents learn how to jointly use and appropriately consume digital media for educational purposes. This will take a step toward narrowing the digital divide, or app gap as some researchers have termed the gap between those children who know how to use digital apps and those who do not. According to *Pioneering Literacy in the Digital Wild West: Empowering Parents and Educators: A Primer for Communities* (Guernsey et al., 2012), a recent report on digital media usage and the potential for helping children demonstrate the ability to achieve grade-level reading success, several areas relating to digital media should be the focus of organizations striving to help all children succeed in literacy development. The four areas identified could be incorporated into the children's library to align with goals for improving the multiliteracies of children and families in the community. These areas, modified specifically for libraries, are:

1 Promoting personal connections among caregivers, teachers, and other educators via social media, texting and the development of "third space" learning communities.

2 Reinforcing basic literacy skills by selecting, evaluating, and making available a variety of digital media in the library such as interactive educational apps, literacy-supportive digital picture books, and online literacy games.

3 Providing opportunities to build background knowledge and foster life-long learning through exciting library services that take advantage of content-rich library materials, museum offerings, e-book services, immersive literacy games interactive multimedia "field trips," and maker spaces.

4 Improving the workforce by providing a space for teachers, family child care providers, and other educators to connect to each other, new resources for literacy instruction and active learning, and professional development opportunities (modified from Guernsey et al., 2012, p. 16).

Notice the emphasis on how digital media are used and the type of environment that is being created. This context is very important when fostering digital literacy. While at an elementary school in Switzerland, Guernsey observed children interacting with iPads in the classroom. Although this scene is mirrored in many affluent classrooms and libraries across the United States, the difference in this European classroom was *how* the iPads were used. Guernsey (2013) recounts,

> The school has an unconventional take on the iPad's purpose. The devices are not really valued as portable screens or mobile gaming devices. Teachers I talked to seemed uninterested, almost dismissive, of animations and gamelike apps. Instead, the tablets were intended to be used as video cameras, audio recorders, and multimedia note-books of individual students' creations. The teachers cared most about how the devices could capture moments that told stories about their students' experiences in school. Instead of focusing on what was coming out of the iPad, they were focused on what was going into it (par. 5).

Notice that the teachers were focusing on the digital literacy development of the children and how they were using digital tablets. The teachers wanted to examine the digital media created by the students to better understand their digital literacy skills and potential for succeeding in our increasingly digital world. The teachers were providing opportunities for active engagement with digital media through developmentally appropriate practices. Gardner and Davis (2013) observe that many children are already tech-savvy and have integrated technology immersion into almost every area of their lives to such an extent that today's digital natives already "think in apps."

As with any type of media for children, moderation is the key. While it is important to foster multiple literacies in digital natives, a media diet for children should include multiple types of print and new digital media as well as a healthy dose of peer socialization and sunshine. The consequences of too much media consumption can be seen in various cautionary tales for children such as the picture book *Penny Lee and Her TV* (McCoy, 2002) demonstrating what happens when a young girl spends all her time in front of the television, and the picture book *Dot.* (Zuckerberg, 2013), which follows a young girl obsessed with her tablet, laptop, and smartphone. Librarians and educators can use both of these books with children and families as conversation starters about media balance. Similarly, *Goodnight iPad* (Droyd, 2011) is a tongue-in-cheek picture book for adults that parodies the children's classic *Goodnight Moon* and emphasizes how media consumption can take over a household. It too can be shared with caregivers, older children, and educators as a way to broach the subject of media overload.

Child psychologist and family therapist Catherine Steiner-Adair also stresses the importance of media moderation for the entire family in her book *The Big Disconnect: Protecting Childhood and Family Relationships in the Digital Age* (2013). Steiner-Adair, along with Theresa Barker, describes numerous accounts of families falling apart because of too much screen time and media consumption. Caregivers can become distracted with their tablets, smartphones, and laptops and fail to bond with their children. At the same time, children do not socialize with their friends, peers, siblings, and other family members in real time because they are mesmerized by the lure of the screen and its promise of staying connected. This breakdown of the family unit is described by Steiner-Adair as indicative of our current age—the Digital Age of Disconnection. She notes, "For every minute or hour your child spends on screens or other digital diversions, he or she is not engaged in healthful, unstructured, creative play" (p. 54).

While critics of children's screen time often place blame on the care-givers, educators, and other adults in children's lives for not moderating their child's media consumption, Stein-Adair observes that in many cases the adults are also the ones who need a media diet. She captures snippets of therapy sessions and interviews with young children where seven-year-olds lament "My mom is almost always on the iPad at dinner. She's always 'just checking'" (p. 12) and "A lot of time at home when my parents are home and on their computers, I feel like I'm not there, because they pretend I'm not there . . . they're like not even talking to me, they just are ignoring me" (p. 13). Consistent digital distraction compromises healthy relation-ships between children and caregivers and between parents. Whenever one person ignores another to answer a text, send an email, and so forth, they are sending the clear message that the technology is more important than the person with them.

> As computers, smartphones, digital tablets, e-readers, and the Internet have become integral components of everyday life, tech has not only sucked us in; it has gained a de facto coparenting role: continuously engaging, informing, entertaining, and mod-eling its digital version of the connected life. If we are too busy to spend time with our kids, too busy to listen to them, or too intimidated or overwhelmed by tech to respond to them, an on-line world of 'intimate strangers' or diversions is ever ready to welcome them (Steiner-Adair and Barker, 2013, p. 18).

In addition to moderating a media diet, it is important to encourage parents to interact and play with their children. Beyond physical play, this also includes digital play—interacting with an app together, reading a digi-tal book collectively, and talking about what is in the illustrations and what is happening on the screen. This is particularly important for families with small children, when it is important to create the initial child-caregiver bond. Similarly, this interaction is essential when fostering cultural competence through digital media. Librarians, teachers, and caregivers should talk with children about the depiction of cultures within a digital app, digital book, or online game; they should talk about any stereotypes that are present and direct the children to other sources about the particular culture; and they should combine digital media with picture books and informational texts

Resources and Reports Describing Digital Media Usage of Children and Families

The Big Disconnect: Protecting Childhood and Family Relationships in the Digital Age. Catherine Steiner-Adair with Teresa H. Barker. New York: Harper, 2013.

Digital Decisions: Choosing the Right Technology Tools for Early Childhood Education. Fran Simon and Karen Nemeth. Lewisville, NC: Gryphon House, 2012.

Families Matter: Designing Media for a Digital Age. Lori M. Takeuchi. New York: The Joan Ganz Cooney Center at Sesame Workshop, 2011. http://www.joanganzcooneycenter.org/wp-content/uploads/2011/06/jgcc_familiesmatter.pdf.

Learning at Home: Families' Educational Media Use in America. Victoria Rideout. New York: The Joan Ganz Cooney Center at Sesame Workshop, 2014. http://www.joanganzcooneycenter.org/wp-content/uploads/2014/01/jgcc_learningathome.pdf.

Pioneering Literacy in the Digital Wild West: Empowering Parents and Educators: A Primer for Communities. Lisa Guernsey, Michael Levine, Cynthia Chiong, and Maggie Severns for the Campaign for Grade-Level Reading. New York: The Joan Ganz Cooney Center at Sesame Workshop and New America Foundation, 2012. http://gradelevelreading.net/wp-content/uploads/2012/12/GLR_TechnologyGuide_final.pdf.

Screen Time: How Electronic Media—From Baby Videos to Educational Software—Affects Your Young Child. Lisa Guernsey. New York: Basic Books, 2012.

Young Children, Apps and iPad. Michael Cohen, Martha Hadley, and Minda Frank. New York: Michael Cohen Group, 2013. http://mcgrc.com/wp-content/uploads/2012/06/ipad-study-cover-page-report-mcg-info_new-online.pdf.

Zero to Eight: Children's Media Use in America 2013. Common Sense Media. New York: Common Sense Media, 2013. http://www.commonsensemedia.org/research/zero-to-eight-childrens-media-use-in-america-2013.

Figure 3.3: Resources and Reports Describing Digital Media Usage of Children and Families

representing diverse cultures to provide multiple perspectives and learning extensions. Kenner (2005) observes that "the few images which make their way into the mainstream media tend to portray minority ethnic communities as trapped in a time-warp of traditionalism" (p. 74). As we discuss later in the book, this "time-warp of traditionalism" is present in the scant, but growing, body of new digital media for children.

In the next chapter we explore librarians' attitudes about digital media in the children's library as well as examples of how current librarians are using digital media with children and their families. Figure 3.3 provides resources for those interested in further readings and additional in-depth resources and reports discussing children and family interaction with various types of digital media.

References

American Academy of Pediatrics, Committee on Public Education. "Media Education." Part 1. *Pediatrics* 104, no. 2 (1999): 341–343.

Anderson, Richard, Elfrieda Hiebert, Judith Scott, and Ian Wilkinson. *Becoming a Nation of Readers: The Report of the Commission on Reading.* Washington, DC: National Institute of Education, 1985.

Gal, Jennifer. (February 14, 2013). "Digital Storytime: Preschool Programming with the iPad." Accessed December 28, 2013, at http://www.slideshare.net/Jennifer.Gal/digital-story-time-sols-feb-14-2013-jennifer-gal.

Gardner, Howard, and Katie Davis. *The App Generation: How Today's Youth Navigate Identity, Intimacy, and Imagination in a Digital World.* New Haven, CT: Yale University Press, 2013.

Greenwalt, R. Toby. "Of Tinkers and Technology: Creative Digital Programming for Youth." *Public Libraries* 52, no. 4 (July/August 2013): 18–20.

Guernsey, Lisa. (April 15, 2013). "The Smart Way to Use iPads in the Classroom." *Slate.* Accessed November 21, 2013, at http://www.slate.com/articles/technology/future_tense/2013/04/ipads_in_the_classroom_the_right_way_to_use_them_demonstrated_by_a_swiss.html.

Guernsey, Lisa. *Screen Time: How Electronic Media—From Baby Videos to Educational Software—Affects Your Young Child.* New York:

Basic Books, 2012. (Originally published as *Into the Minds of Babes: How Screen Time Affects Children from Birth to Age Five*. New York: Basic Books, 2007.)

Guernsey, Lisa, and Michael Levine. (December 13, 2012). "Educational Apps Alone Won't Teach Your Child to Read." *Slate*. Accessed November 21, 2013, at http://www.slate.com/blogs/future_tense/2012/12/13/kids_apps_and_e-books_can_t_teach_them_to_read_without_parent_and_teacher.html.

Guernsey, Lisa, Michael Levine, Cynthia Chiong, and Maggie Severns. (2012). *Pioneering Literacy in the Digital Wild West: Empowering Parents and Educators: A Primer for Communities*. New York: The Joan Ganz Cooney Center at Sesame Workshop and New America Foundation. Accessed December 30, 2013, at http://gradelevelreading.net/wp-content/uploads/2012/12/GLR_TechnologyGuide_final.pdf.

Herr-Stephenson, B., M. Alper, E. Reilly, and H. Jenkins. (2013). *T Is for Transmedia: Learning Through Transmedia Play*. Los Angeles and New York: USC Annenberg Innovation Lab and the Joan Ganz Cooney Center at Sesame Workshop. Accessed November 21, 2013, at http://www.annenberglab.com/viewresearch/46.

Hopwood, Jennifer. (June 8, 2013). "The Gamification of Reading." *ALSC Blog*. Accessed January 1, 2014, at http://www.alsc.ala.org/blog/2013/06/the-gamification-of-reading/.

Institute of Museum and Library Services. (2013). *Growing Young Minds: How Museums and Libraries Create Lifelong Learners*. Washington, DC: Institute of Museum and Library Services. Accessed February 28, 2014, at http://www.imls.gov/assets/1/AssetManager/GrowingYoungMinds.pdf.

Jenkins, Henry. (2013). "Introduction." In *T Is for Transmedia: Learning Through Transmedia Play* (pp. 4–9). Los Angeles and New York: USC Annenberg Innovation Lab and the Joan Ganz Cooney Center at Sesame Workshop. Accessed December 28, 2013, at http://www.annenberglab.com/viewresearch/46.

Kenner, Charmian. "Bilingual Children's Uses of Popular Culture in Text-Making." In *Popular Culture, New Media and Digital Literacy in Early Childhood*, ed. by Jackie Marsh (pp. 73–87). London: Routledge, 2005.

Mackey, Margaret. "The New Basics: Learning to Read in a Multimedia World." *English in Education* 28, no. 1 (1994): 9–19.

National Association for the Education of Young Children (NAEYC). *Technology and Young Children—Ages 3 Through 8*. Position Statement. Washington, DC: NAEYC, 1996.

National Association for the Education of Young Children and the Fred Rogers Center for Early Learning and Children's Media. (January 2012). *Technology and Interactive Media as Tools in Early Childhood Programs Serving Children from Birth Through Age 8*. Joint position statement. Washington, DC: NAEYC; Latrobe, PA: Fred Rogers Center for Early Learning and Children's Media. Accessed December 28, 2013, at http://www.naeyc.org/content/technology-and-young-children.

Neuman, Susan B., and Donna C. Celano. *Giving Our Children a Fighting Chance: Poverty, Literacy, and the Development of Information Capital*. New York: Teachers College Press, 2012.

Pew Research Center. (December 11, 2013). *How Americans Value Public Libraries in Their Communities*. Accessed December 21, 2013, at http://libraries.pewinternet.org/2013/12/11/libraries-in-communities/.

Steiner-Adair, Catherine, and Teresa H. Barker. *The Big Disconnect: Protecting Childhood and Family Relationships in the Digital Age*. New York: Harper, 2013.

Unsworth, Len, Angela Thomas, Alyson Simpson, and Jennifer Asha. *Children's Literature and Computer Based Teaching*. Maidenhead, Berkshire (England): Open University Press, 2005.

Children's Books

Droyd, Ann. *Goodnight iPad: A Parody for the New Generation*. New York: Blue Rider Press/Penguin, 2011.

McCoy, Glenn. *Penny Lee and Her TV*. New York: Hyperion Books for Children, 2002.

Zuckerberg, Randi. *Dot*. Illus. by Joe Berger. New York: HarperCollins, 2013.

Chapter 4

Digital Media in the Children's Library

> The virtual explosion in [book] apps has transformed the traditional storybook of early childhood into a highly interactive, multi-media literacy experience (Roskos et al., 2014, p. 1).

> You wouldn't dream of substituting a touch-screen meal for real food, and no matter how sophisticated voice tech becomes, audio or digital books and reading games are no substitute for personally reading to your [child] (Steiner-Adair and Barker, 2013 pp. 88–89).

When using new digital media with children and families in library programs, it is important to remember that new digital media are meant to *supplement* not *replace* print books, songs, and hand-on activities usually found in the children's library. Rather, digital apps and digital picture books should enhance and extend the learning ongoing in library programming, providing a highly interactive multiliteracy experience. It is important to progressively add digital content to children's programming and consistently update your knowledge of the various options available. Equally important is selecting the best digital media to inspire learning. In Chapter 6 we detail various criteria for selecting the best digital media that will keep children actively engaged and promote cultural competence.

Simon and Nemeth (2012) advise that the use of digital media should not overshadow the educator, noting "When you decide to use technology in your [library program], it should be so well integrated that it will not even stand out among the other experiences you offer every day. It will become a part of the fabric of your [program] culture and practices"

(p. 31). Again, the key is selecting and using developmentally appropriate digital media and using them correctly. Digital media should not be a passive replacement for activity and social interaction. Instead, digital media should be interactive, educational, and skill building. In fact, research studies indicate that interactive digital picture books and apps can help increase early literacy skill development in children, particularly those from lower socioeconomic backgrounds (Korat and Shamir, 2007; Roskos et al., 2014). When married with culturally sensitive, early literacy activities that typically occur in children's library programming, the potential for skill building is even greater—as is the prospect for fostering cultural literacy.

For specific considerations for integrating digital media in the children's library see Figure 4.1.

Children's Librarians' Opinions on Digital Media in Library Programs

We would be remiss if we did not capture the ongoing discussion among children's librarians surrounding the potential of and apprehensions about using new digital media in the children's library. As with most issues of importance, there is a spectrum of viewpoints. There are the polarized librarians who either believe there is no place for digital media in the library or who vociferously support its inclusion as a vital part of the children's library. At the same time, there are librarians who fall somewhere in the middle and believe that digital media in moderation have a place in the library. According to Nemeth and Campbell (2013), "Children's librarians are leaders in using new media with young children. They are up-to-date with recent e-books and apps and how to incorporate those tools into traditional early literacy programming. Since librarians are trained experts in evaluating and curating reading materials, they can help others find and use the best apps, websites, and software . . . " (p. 28). While this statement may be true for some self-motivated children's librarians, does it reflect the majority of current children's librarians? Are we up-to-date with new digital media and do we use them in our library programming? Or are these goals that we are striving toward?

In December 2013 the Digital Media Diet, a blog discussing the use of digital media with children, provided a current snapshot of the debate about screen time for children, emphasizing the importance of children's high-quality interactions with apps. In response to the article, youth librarian Genesis Hansen commented, "There are too [sic] very entrenched ex-

Recommendations for Integrating Digital Media in the Children's Library to Promote Cultural Competence

- Integrate digital media about various cultural groups into regular weekly, monthly, and special programs.

- Have a clear purpose and objective for using digital media in library programming. The digital media should be supportive of the themes in the program and not an "add on" or time filler.

- Utilize apps and other digital media that create deeper learning experiences for the children to explore various cultures through interactive engagement and play.

- Choose apps and other digital media that support multiple learning styles and explore a variety of aspects about a particular culture or cultures.

- Create a balance of librarian-led activities (in both small and large groups) with digital media and individualized child independent activities.

- Resist the urge to select "cutesy" apps and digital media that perpetuate cultural stereotypes. No matter how visually appealing or cute the digital media, if they provide misinformation then their usefulness in promoting cultural competence is compromised.

Figure 4.1: Recommendations for Integrating Digital Media in the Children's Library to Promote Cultural Competence, loosely adapted and expanded from Simon and Nemeth (2012)

tremes around this issue: those who are thoughtlessly exposing children to digital media of all kinds, using those media as babysitters rather than engagement tools, etc. and those who are reacting against media use with the extreme response of 'no screens, ever'" (2013, par. 2). Hansen goes on to explain that while some librarians and educators want to put a time limit on digital media use, she believes that quality time, not the quantity of time is the important consideration. What children are doing with an app (the level of engagement and learning opportunities) is an important consideration. Hansen suggests that more time with an educational app is better than less time with an app without purpose.

In January 2013 Cen Campbell, children's librarian and founder of Little eLit: Early Literacy in the Digital Age (http://littleelit.com/), sent a message to the discussion list of the Association for Library Service to Children (ALSC-L) as an open invitation and call to action for children's librarians to embrace the use of apps in storytime programs and within the children's library. In this message she chided librarians for being unwilling to accept changes in technology and educational use, stating: "The children's library community is WAY [sic] behind ECE [early childhood education] educators, researchers and administrators in making use of mobile tech with young kids; we are not trailblazing here, we are catching up to the rest of the world's current media use" (Online Communication, January 22, 2013, par. 3). Campbell went on to give librarians a pep talk about the role they could play in digital literacy education, commenting: "We are in the middle of a format-based sea-change that spans far beyond libraryland and into publishing, pedagogy, multi-literacies, special needs education, diversity and federal and state policy. It's a much bigger phenomenon than many librarians realize, yet there is no better profession to step in and make recommendations on the intelligent use of book-based and educational apps with children" (Online Communication, January 22, 2013, par. 4). The responses she received from fellow children's librarians were quite varied. One outspoken children's librarian and author from Oregon vehemently denounced the use of digital media in storytime programs and Campbell's "either do it or die" post, commenting,

> Many libraries don't have the funds to present high tech, or even low tech storytimes. Many librarians are unable to find the time to become as highly trained as others because they are the only ones at the library. Many librarians feel uncomfortable about promoting apps as part of storytime for ethical reasons, but they offer dynamite storytimes that include early literacy tips, which might focus once in a while on giving brief advice to parents about apps and screen time. Many librarians are still not sure that apps and screens at storytime aren't a contradiction to our message. (Online Communication, January 22, 2013, par. 4)

A library director from Texas noted that he did not have a problem with using digital apps in storytimes but that it should not be a "must do" activity. Rather, the children's librarian should choose whatever tools and methods he thought was necessary to deliver a dynamic storytime experience. Another librarian from Louisiana concurred, stating that although she was not a fan of technology, "We should all do the best that we can to make storytimes and all of our programs meaningful. If having an 'app' storytime brings in patrons then go for it! If patrons prefer a traditional storytime, wonderful! It doesn't have to be all or nothing" (Online Communication, January 23, 2013, par. 2). A librarian from Iowa further noted that before children's librarians adopt apps into storytimes, more information and research should be made available about the benefits of using the technology with three- and four-year-old children. She also went on to suggest that using apps in storytimes would take away from the "shared experience" of everyone involved. In response to this post, a librarian from Ohio commented that using an app in storytime was no different than using a flannel board or draw-and-tell story — an app was just another mode for delivering content. One final librarian from Connecticut shared examples and photos of digital storytime programs that she has hosted or observed, stating, "We, as professionals, can choose where and how we support the computer and digital literacy development of our families in ways that are appropriate for our program and community" (Online Communication, January 23, 2013, par. 6).

Six months later, Kathy Kleckner (2013), a children's librarian in the Dakota County Library System (Minnesota), strongly opposed the use of digital tablets in library storytimes in her ALSC Blog post "The Screen Free Story Time Is the Best Story Time." Kleckner emphasizes the role of the library in promoting early literacy development and stresses that screens have no place in helping young children learn in the library. She provides a list of six reasons why traditional storytime practices, such as rhymes and fingerplays, puppetry, hands-on manipulatives, and reading from print books, are much better than digital tablets in the library. A few days later, Carisa Kluver (2013), creator of the Digital Storytime app review website, provided a counter argument to Kleckner's assertions on the Digital Media Diet blog. She noted that the public library is there to serve all people in the community, meeting their literacy, educational, and informational needs using a variety of methods. Kluver suggests that librarians who resist embracing technology use with young children are doing a disservice to their local patron base. She also lists six reasons why digital tablets in the library may increase children's early literacy skills.

In September 2013 Cen Campbell sent another message to ALSC-L asking children's librarians for suggestions on what they thought was necessary in a new toolkit for librarians wanting to integrate new digital media into library programs and collections. She received only one public response to her post. A Minnesota librarian was open to the idea but suggested, "There is a dire need for library professionals to have a knowledge base that will support decision-making, communications, practices, and guiding principles to the benefit of the children and parents we serve" (Online Communication, September 14, 2013, par. 1). She then went on to describe almost twenty areas for consideration, ranging from the role of new digital media in school readiness and success to the influence that new digital media have in the relationship between children and their caregivers. While Campbell may have received other posts or tweets privately, this public post, compared with the public posts she received just nine months earlier, seemed to suggest that some children's librarians are ready to put personal and pedagogical opinions aside and have the necessary discussion about how the children's library fits into the world of digital media. Certainly, now is the time to have these discussions! In February 2014 almost fifty children's librarians and children's librarian educators engaged in a lengthy online discussion via the ALSC listserv about the use of real versus virtual sock puppets in storytime programs, debating the use of a sock puppet app rather than a physical puppet to engage children. One librarian from Minnesota described the discussion as research-guided practice versus commercially driven practice, stating:

> The practice of app use as content or "technique" to support child development and literacy is unproven and the idea that app use is no different than traditional materials is an assumption. Yet we do have research showing that screen time is associated with a number of problems for children. What educators recommend modeling unproven, marginal or risk-related behaviors?

> "I use apps for only a minute," you might say. Corporations pay millions for one minute of time. It is the message that counts and the message is the medium. Who benefits from this message? We do not know that children and families will benefit. There are numerous reasons to believe they won't. Isn't it indisputable that tech companies will benefit from librarians promoting apps? It is not an accident that app marketing to librarians is centered in Silicon Valley.

> If librarians do not fully appreciate and value what research offers us and the dangers of ignorance then I don't see how we can expect anyone in the world to do so. This bothers me. How about you? (Online Communication, February 14, 2014, par. 3–5)

While librarians such as the one above are stringently opposed to the use of apps with children, others are sharing their innovative ideas for incorporating digital media into their children's departments. Little eLit has been compiling ideas, examples, and story plans for some time now, representing a growing archive of digital media activities in libraries across the United States. In addition, the ALSC blog has featured several posts in recent years with examples of how children's librarians incorporate digital media into storytimes, profile digital children's media on their library websites, provide app advisory services to parents, create interactive iPad stations, and more. To explore these testimonials and other examples of digital media in the children's library, see Figure 4.2. For an interview with Cen Campbell about digital media usage in the children's library, see Figure 4.3.

Digital Storytime Logistics

Librarians interested in integrating digital media into children's programs may initially feel intimidated and unsure where to turn. Fortunately, Cen Campbell and her colleagues at Little eLit have created an amazing website (http://littleelit.com/) with recommendations for selecting apps, suggestions for software and hardware specifics, and sample digital storytime program plans. While a discussion on the specific hardware and software needed for a digital storytime is essential for librarians beginning these programs, we understand that equipment is constantly changing and being updated. Therefore we will provide a high-level overview of what is needed for a digital storytime and refer librarians to Little eLit for the most up-to-date information. Basic items needed for a digital storytime include: multiple digital tablets (such as iPads), a tablet protector case (such as The Survivor), tablet screen protectors, an LCD projector, a large screen, HDMI or VGA cable to project tablet content onto the screen, an iTunes or Google Play account to download apps, access to cloud software to allow sharing on up to eight mobile devices (smartphones or tablets), and charging stations. Another consideration is the type of digital device to use with the children. Most digital storytimes use digital tablets, but other devices can be used in library programming such as iPods and tabletop touch screen computers. Depending on the particular digital app or digital picture book used, the level of interactivity, and the amount of librarian interaction, a touch screen computer might be better than a digital tablet and vice versa. When using book apps, specific multi-sensory behaviors in young children (such as listening, looking, touching, moving, gesturing, making noises, and

Examples of Digital Media in the Children's Library

About Apps and Autism (http://www.alsc.ala.org/blog/2013/03/about-apps-and-autism/)—Barbara Klipper, Librarian, Stamford, CT, discusses in depth the tremendous potential for specific digital apps to help children with autism spectrum disorder and how these can be incorporated into the children's library.

App Advisory for Parents (http://www.alsc.ala.org/blog/2013/10/app-advisory-for-parents/)—Liz Fraser, children's librarian/technology coordinator in Lake Zurich, IL, describes an "Appy Hour" complete with appetizers and lists of recommended digital apps for parents.

Apps with Curriculum (http://appswithcurriculum.com/)—Cyndie Sebourn, author and retired teacher, provides curriculum guides, reviews, and recommendations for connecting apps in the school curriculum and various standards including Common Core.

Cherokee Language Technology Program (http://ailanet.org/events/cherokee-language-technologythe-syllabary-and-the-nations-history-of-technological-adoption/)—Roy Boney Jr., language technologist for the Cherokee Nation Education Services Group, briefly describes an Institute of Museum and Library Services (IMLS) project that uses Cherokee language apps with young Cherokee language learners in tribal libraries and community centers to help the new generation learn their native language.

Circulating iPads in the Children's Library (http://www.alsc.ala.org/blog/2011/11/circulating-ipads-in-the-childrens-library/)—Kiera Parrot, librarian, Darien Public Library, CT, provides in-depth information about the library's circulating collection of Early Literacy iPad Kits.

Digital Resources on Library Websites for Kids (http://www.alsc.ala.org/blog/2013/02/digital-resources-on-library-websites-for-kids-2/)—Paige

facial expression) are expressed differently depending on the digital device (Roskos et al., 2014).

In addition to using the digital tablets in storytimes, some libraries mount the tablets on the end of shelf caps in the library. This forms a kiosk that allows librarians to have an "App of the Day" available for children to explore. Typically, the mounting hardware covers access to settings so patrons cannot disable the featured app. The perk to having such a kiosk is the ability to feature a diverse array of apps (educational, gaming, and story), including culturally inclusive apps that allow children to explore

Bentley-Flannery, children's/community librarian, Deschutes Public Library, OR, compiles a list of noteworthy children's library websites that profile digital media for children, including digital picture-book subscription services such as BookFlix and TumbleBooks.

Digital Scavenger Hunt (http://www.alsc.ala.org/blog/2013/10/digital-scavenger-hunt/)—Claire Moore, assistant head of children's services, Darien Public Library, CT, shares how she created a successful digital scavenger hunt using digital apps to reinforce digital literacy skills covered in her weekly tech class for tweens.

Digital Storytime: Preschool Programming with the iPad (http://www.slideshare.net/Jennifer.Gal/digital-story-time-sols-feb-14-2013-jennifer-gal)—Jennifer Gal, librarian, Hamilton Public Library, Hamilton, Canada, describes the basics for incorporating digital media into storytime programs for young children.

"iPads for Everyone: How a Small Library Program Became a Runaway Hit and Reached More Than 4,100 Kids and Teachers." (October 2012, The Digital Shift, *School Library Journal*) (http://www.thedigitalshift.com/2012/10/ebooks/ipads-for-everyone-how-a-small-library-program-became-a-runaway-hit-and-reached-more-than-4100-kids-and-teachers/)—Carolyn Foote, school librarian, Westlake High School, Austin, TX, notes how she incorporated iPads into the daily educational environment of her high school. Although the focus is for young adults, Foote's ideas could be applied to the children's library.

Touch and Learn Hour—A Digital Non-Fiction Story Time (http://www.alsc.ala.org/blog/2013/11/touch-and-learn-hour-a-digital-non-fiction-story-time/)—Emily Scherrer, youth services manager, Yuma County Library District, AZ, details how she incorporates digital media such as e-books and apps into a grant-funded program promoting STEM learning. The activities she describes could also be used by school librarians to meet Common Core Standards.

Figure 4.2: Examples of Digital Media in the Children's Library

various traditions of other children around the globe. The Dixon (CA) Public Library provides an extensive guide for librarians who are considering implementing an iPad program. This guide (available at http://littleelit.com/2014/01/13/preliminary-guide-to-the-ipad-program-at-dixon-public-library/) includes information on policies and procedures for both librarian and patron use, maintenance and security suggestions, and ideas for classification and collection development.

Text continues on page 72

Getting Digital in the Children's Library with Cen Campbell

Cen Campbell is a vivacious and passionate librarian working at both the local and national levels to train librarians on how to purposefully use new digital media in children's library programs. She has worked in both Canadian and U.S. libraries and is the founder of Little eLit, an extensive blog and Web resource capturing the current journey of children's librarians and library advocates as they incorporate digital media into daily library practices. If there is breaking news or advancement in new media for young children, Cen usually has her finger in the mix or is closely connected with a digital literacy expert involved.

Digital Media, Children, and the Library

While Cen's enthusiasm for using digital media in children's library programming is infectious, she has also met her share of resistance from concerned librarians and educators. These concerns range from the fear that digital media may be developmentally inappropriate for young children to anxiety about media taking over books in the library. Cen understands this trepidation but believes the worries are indicative of recurring problems in early childhood education and librarianship. In the past, some librarians were worried about the use of graphic novels, DVDs, video games, Lego blocks, etc., in children's programs. Those fears have been assuaged and eventually, Cen hopes, the panic relating to the inclusion of digital media (such as apps) will disappear as librarians become more educated about their use with children. She firmly believes that "Apps are just the technology of the day, and it's becoming less and less important to be an expert in a particular type of device or format. Being able to pick up and learn new technologies and adapt to the changing needs of the families who are surrounded by those technologies is a much more important skill, but it's a huge paradigm shift for a lot of librarians."

Cen believes that children's librarians should incorporate digital media into all collections, services, and programs for young children and cites a number of reasons for this. Specifically, she asserts:

1 Digital reading is a legitimate reading choice for many families. Librarians help bring the right resources to the right people at the right time, and increasingly some of those resources are digital, even for the youngest of children.

2 There is a great need for curation and reader's advisory services in the children's digital media marketplace. If librarians don't offer guidance in this area, content developers and those with a commercial stake will fill the void.

3 Adoption rates for mobile technology are increasing exponentially; children have access to these devices already. Why not provide parents with recommendations for high-quality, age-appropriate content?

4 The digital divide is alive and well, and we're now seeing that providing access to technology alone does not bridge the digital divide. Rather, it can exacerbate it as Susan Neuman and Donna Celano point out in their eye-opening *Giving Our Children a Fighting Chance: Poverty, Literacy, and the Information Capital*. Librarians can support the development of information capital in at-risk communities by intentionally and appropriately using new media in programming for young children in libraries.

Cen acknowledges that there *can* be risks in using digital media with young children, particularly when they are used inappropriately. Chip Donohue at the Technology in Early Childhood Center at the Erikson Institute in Chicago points out various concerns relating to using screen media with young children. These include: overexposure to harmful commercialization, shortened attention spans, decrease in social interaction, disruption of sleep cycles, and limited exposure to outdoor activities. But Cen notes that Chip also describes how to use what we do know about child development and media literacy to make the best use of technology. She points to Lisa Guernsey's 3 C's—content, context, and child—as a way to approach digital media usage with children and states, "I find it a little strange to apply a medical, risk-based frame to a pedagogical tool, but I think the key is moderation. Of course there are risks when a child plays with an iPad for hours on end by him or herself, but there are risks when a young child does *anything* for hours on end by him or herself. I think the 'risks' that often concern people have more to do with overconsumption, parental engagement and inappropriate content than the medium itself."

According to Cen, literacy scholars, pedagogues, pediatricians, and child advocates from around the world are examining the effects of interactive and screen media on children with new information being made available on a continual basis. "I am not a researcher in this area, nor am I a technophile searching for ways to push technology into our children's chubby little hands at all costs," Cen concedes. "I am

Figure 4.3 continues on page 70

a children's librarian responding to the needs of families with young children who are navigating the realities of the digital era, and I must rely on the recommendations of such qualified bodies as the American Academy of Pediatrics, the National Association for the Education of Young Children, Common Sense Media, and even tech-averse groups like the Campaign for a Commercial Free Childhood." Based on the recommendations from these organizations, Cen observes the following:

1   When used intentionally and appropriately, technology and interactive media are effective tools to support learning and development. (NAEYC, 2012)

2   The American Academy of Pediatrics continues to be concerned by evidence about the potential harmful effects of media messages and images; however, important positive and prosocial effects of media use should also be recognized. (AAP, 2013)

3   Not all screens are created equal. (Common Sense Media)

4   Research tells us that developing children thrive when they are talked to, read to, played with, and given time for creative play, physically active play, and interactions with other children and adults. (Campaign for a Commercial-Free Childhood et al., 2012)

Often the concerns that arise about the damaging effects of screen time and media usage have more to do with vast quantities of background media than interactive media use. Cen suggests, "Reading a Sandra Boynton book in app form or using Doodlecast to create a story as part of a storytime is not the same as watching hours of Sponge Bob Square Pants (Not all screens are created equal!). To me this question of screen time has less to do with technology and more to do with moderation and common sense. Here are two of my own guidelines:

1   The use of new media with young children should be a focal point for interaction and a springboard for further discussion or activities.

2   New media incorporated into a program for young children should be intentional and age-appropriate."

Cen goes on to remark, "The question about media use with children under 2 often arises in these discussions. First of all, children this age don't *need* media to learn. They need interaction, but that interaction can be supported or even facilitated with the use of new media. Sometimes the discussion devolves into an either-or proposition like 'there's no app for going outside.' We don't have to choose. We can do both. The reality is that children under the age of two do use different forms of media (often tablet based). At the very least, librarians can tell parents that what their child needs to do most is talk, sing, read, write, and play with loving caregivers, and show them ways to do that while using a smartphone or tablet. For storytime purposes we can't forget that the program is just as much for the parents as it is for the child; using new media (like nursery rhyme apps, or posting lyrics for unfamiliar songs that they can access online later) can support the parents in their role as their child's first and best teacher by supporting them to learn new techniques for engaging with their children."

When concerns about using digital tablets in children's library programs for young children arise in Cen's workshops, she often asks librarians how many have used a PowerPoint presentation, Smart Board, or scanned versions of physical books, or posted or suggested videos of fingerplays on YouTube to help parents remember the words. She almost always receives exclamations of "Oh! I never thought of it like that!" around the room. "We're already doing this! Librarians sometimes just get stuck on the format, and in the process short-change the potential for facilitating a dynamic and compelling learning experience for the parents," Cen emphasizes. "We librarians sometimes run around in circles trying to figure out what to do with the format of a package of information, and we often allow the format to trump the quality or age appropriateness of the content. At the same time, this most recent generation of kids are just reading in any and every format they can. They are format agnostic. They may prefer one type of digital book over another, or be more drawn to reading materials that incorporate some kind of gamification, and some of them will prefer the feel of a paper book. Digital books don't replace traditional storytelling techniques and tools; that's like saying that puppets replace fingerplays. The intentional and appropriate use of digital media is a boon to any storyteller's toolkit. As more and more books (or whatever the new incarnation is—apps are here today but who knows what the next format will be) are published digitally, it'll become increasingly important for librarians to incorporate them into all services, collections, and programs for families with young children. Our storytime should reflect the publishing marketplace, and that marketplace is becoming increasingly digital."

Little eLit and the Curation of Digital Storytimes

Since establishing Little eLit in November 2011 Cen has noticed distinct changes in the landscape. Increasingly more librarians are using new media in their storytimes and reporting what they've learned on Little eLit. As a result, more questions about protective cases and circulation policies for digital tablets have appeared on the ALSC (Association for

Figure 4.3 continues on page 72

Library Service to Children) and PUBYAC listservs, and through the contact form on Little eLit. There are also more libraries investing in tablets and staff training and more conference presentations on best apps for kids.

Cen remarks, "Lots of librarians and library systems contact me personally with questions, but these days I'm often not the best person to answer troubleshooting device or app-specific questions. We've got a fantastic think tank of forward-thinking, motivated children's librarians who work together to figure out the answers and then share

Text continued from page 67

If children and families fully embrace incorporating digital apps into literacy learning and play, then they may want to take digital tablets home to explore further. One of the best resources for how to create a circulating collection of digital tablets in the children's library is Darien (CT) Public Library. The library is a forerunner in embracing digital media in programming and in the collection and has created circulating Early Literacy iPad Kits for families. According to librarian Kiera Parrott (2011), each kit includes the following:

◊ An iPad pre-loaded with librarian-selected apps geared towards pre-readers

◊ An annotated list of the librarian-selected apps

◊ Tips and information on what makes a great app for children and how parents can find more

◊ A fact sheet on screen time and how touchscreen technology can be used with young children

◊ A list of further resources (including books, articles, and websites) on technology and children

◊ Detailed instructions on using the library's OverDrive collection to download e-books and digital audiobooks

◊ A survey to gauge how and why families are using the kits and what improvements they might like to see

Since the inception of the program in September 2011, several of Darien Public's librarians have presented nationally about the success of the program. Just two months after the program launched, Parrott (2011) observed that the kits have a "holds queue of at least 40 patrons long at any

them around. I've gone from being the only blogger, reporting back on my experiments in my own storytimes, to leaving the everyday runnlng of the blog to our talented and lovely editor, Amy Koester, while I work toward national training and advocacy campaigns around the role of the children's librarian in the digital age. People do report back that Little eLit.com has been helpful to them, and it's incredibly gratifying to know that our specialized little library blog is reaching folks who are looking for information on this rather amorphous and quickly changing topic." For additional information on Cen's work, consult: http://littleelit.com/.

Figure 4.3: Getting Digital in the Children's Library with Cen Campbell

given time. We have not yet had to worry about storing the kits, since they are always checked out."

It appears that the program is still successful. We checked the staying power of this statistic by doing a random check of the library's iPad Kit holdings in December 2013 and discovered that two years after the program began the popularity is holding strong—all six iPad Kits were either checked out or on the hold shelf, with 36 additional requests (holds) placed for the kits. Further information about the Darien Library's Early Literacy iPad Kits can be found on the library's website (http://www.darienlibrary.org/youth/elipads).

Information for librarians about children's digital media usage for educational purposes is changing at an exponential rate, with new reports appcaring almost weekly. To keep abreast of these changes, it is recommended that librarians consult the following online resources: *School Library Journal's* The Digital Shift (http://www.thedigitalshift.com/), The Digital Media Diet (http://digitalmediadiet.com/), Little eLit (http://littleelit.com/), and the Children's Book Council's New in Digital (http://www.cbcbooks.org/category/new-in-digital/).

Concluding Thoughts: Babies and Bathwater

We've talked about the various types of digital media, the ongoing discussion around the use of digital media with children, and how librarians are integrating digital media in the children's library. We have purposefully waited until now to look at the recent statistics regarding digital media usage of children and their families. Why? We wanted to explain why the use

Text continues on page 76

Digital Media "On the Loose" in Library Storytimes with Betsy Diamant-Cohen

In the late 1980s while in Israel, children's librarian and storyteller Betsy Diamant-Cohen crafted Mother Goose on the Loose (MGOL), a dynamic, research-based early-literacy program for libraries serving young children ages birth to three and their caregivers. The interactive program incorporates repetition and music to reinforce learning and model literacy activities for caregivers to explore with their young children. MGOL made its U.S. debut in 1998 at the Enoch Pratt Free Library (MD) and later Betsy took the program on the road through various library-training workshops around the country. In 2006 she published *Mother Goose on the Loose: A Handbook and CD-Rom Kit with Scripts, Rhymes, Songs, Flannel-Board Patterns, and Activities for Promoting Early Childhood Development* (Neal-Schuman, 2006) as a way to share her programming principles with librarians around the world. Later she developed and shared a Spanish-language version of the program, *Early Literacy Programming en Español: Mother Goose on the Loose for Bilingual Learners* (Neal-Schuman, 2010) along with music CDs in English, Hebrew, and Spanish. In 2013 MGOL went digital with the development of *Felt Board Mother Goose on the Loose*, named one of 50 Best New Educational Apps by iTunes during its first week of availability. Reminiscent of an actual felt board with manipulative pieces, this engaging creative app encourages young children and their caregivers to explore nursery rhymes, storytelling, and more through repetition, child-parent bonding, and interactive play.

While some critics and researchers believe that screen time with young children can have a negative impact on a child's development, Betsy believes this relates more to TV screen time rather than to interaction with digital media such as digital apps. "Exposure to digital media has to be appropriate," she notes. "Technology should not be used as a babysitter. Book apps and learning apps hold potential for early literacy learning when they promote parent-child bonding and the social skills necessary for healthy child development." Although there is currently hysteria in children's librarianship that new media will replace books in storytimes, Betsy affirms that children's librarians can use digital media to enhance and expand programming and literacy learning without overshadowing the power of books. She states, "Technology is out there and whether we like it or not parents are still going to use it with their young children. Children's librarians cannot stick their heads in the sand and pretend it does not exist. We have to embrace the new media and take the opportunity to guide parents on how to appropriately use digital media with their children to promote healthy development and learning opportunities. Despite all the technology available, the fact that we are still using flannel boards in library programming says something."

The physical flannel board traditionally used in library storytimes creates a happy, positive environment for children learning literacy skills through song and

Felt Board Mother Goose on the Loose app by Betsy Diamant-Cohen

story reading. Betsy believes that the digital flannel board such as the one in the *MGOL* app holds the same potential for creating a positive environment where children and caregivers play and explore songs together to develop not only traditional early literacy skills but also digital literacy skills such as swiping, tapping, and navigation. She stresses that book and learning apps should not be about mastering levels to succeed and receive rewards or gratification. Rather, she believes good apps such as *MGOL* teach children to use language, humor, and creative play and storytelling to solve problems. Problem solving is part of STEM learning and contributes to the development of 21st-century skills or multiliteracies. The *MGOL* app also includes an extensive parent section that provides an avenue to experience the app and rhymes and gives rich suggestions for hands-on learning opportunities that extend the rhymes through manipulatives, reading, creative play, and more, all outside the context of the digital app.

In the "MGOL & New Media" section of the Mother Goose on the Loose website (http://www.mgol.net/about/mgol-and-technology/mgol-and-new-media/), Betsy also provides multiple examples of how new media can be incorporated to extend skills learning and enrich the activities in traditional MGOL storytime programs. These include using SmartBoards to show colors, playing complementary music on iPads, developing and sharing videos of children singing using an LCD projector and a screen, and inviting children to manipulate shapes and characters on the *MGOL Felt Board* app. Betsy suggests that librarians can use the *MGOL* app in storytime, model its use with caregivers, foster early literacy learning, and then allow the child and caregiver to explore on their own what has been modeled. She believes in the potential of

Figure 4.4 continues on page 76

using digital media appropriately in storytimes (with books of course) to such an extent that she has created a new workshop series with Cen Campbell entitled Goose 2.0: Incorporating Digital Media into Mother Goose on the Loose. The workshop introduces librarians to different types of new media, examines evaluation of apps for children, discusses policy statements and issues facing technology use with children, demonstrates how age-appropriate digital media can complement (but not replace) the standard use of rhymes, songs, puppets, musical instruments, and felt boards in library storytimes, and offers tips on guiding parents toward healthy "technology behavior" for youngsters.

Betsy also recognizes the potential of digital media to promote cultural literacy and sees her *MGOL* app as a nonthreatening way to explore the merger of cultures through Spanish-language songs and racially di-

Text continued from page 73

of digital media in the children's library works and what it offers today's digital natives. The following statistics serve to emphasize that children and their families are using digital media now more than ever and that avenues exist for libraries to facilitate learning opportunities with digital media.

- In 2013, 67 percent of children ages 2–13 with Internet access read an e-book and 92 percent of those children consumed e-books at least once a week (Bryant, 2014).

- In 2013, more than a quarter (28 percent) of children ages 0–8 had read an e-book or had one read to them (Common Sense Media, 2013).

- In 2012, almost half (46 percent) of children ages 6–17 had read an e-book, up from 25 percent in 2010 (Scholastic, 2013).

- In 2012, 80 percent of children ages 6–17 who read e-books still read books in print (Scholastic, 2013).

- In 2013, 72 percent of children ages 0–8 had used a mobile device for media activity, up from 38 percent in 2011. Similarly, 38 percent of children ages 0–2 had used a mobile device for media activity, up from 10 percent in 2011 (Common Sense Media, 2013).

- In 2013, 50 percent of children ages 0–8 had used mobile apps, up from16 percent in 2011 (Common Sense Media, 2013).

verse nursery rhyme characters. In the original printed version of MGOL, little cultural diversity was present in the illustrations and manipulative patterns. When she produced the Spanish-language version of the program, Betsy included more diversity in terms of content and hired Evelio Méndez to record Spanish versions of the rhymes. With the *MGOL* app, a playful atmosphere is created for children to explore Spanish and English versions of the Eency Weency Spider and interact with nursery characters that could be seen as African American, Latino, Asian American, Caucasian, or bicultural. Through creative play, Betsy believes that children can explore cross-cultural relationships in Jack and Jill and learn Spanish words and phrases through song. Additional information about the MGOL programs, books, workshops, and app is available at http://www.mgol.net.

Figure 4.4: Digital Media "On the Loose" in Library Storytimes with Betsy Diamant-Cohen

◊ In 2013, 20 percent of lower-income families had a tablet compared with 63 percent of higher-income families (Common Sense Media, 2013).

◊ 35 percent of lower-income parents in 2013 had downloaded educational apps for their children compared with 49 percent of middle-income parents and 75 percent of higher-income ones (Common Sense Media, 2013).

◊ "Recent studies conducted by the Pew Hispanic Center and by independent scholars have found that for many low-income and Hispanic adults, cell phones are the preferred or only means of accessing the Internet and engaging in online searches"(Guernsey et al., 2012, p. 19).

◊ "Recent studies are also documenting that Hispanic and African American families are adopting new digital devices such as tablets for family communication and knowledge acquisition" (Guernsey et al., 2012, p. 20).

How do these statistics influence children's librarians? More and more children are reading e-books but still enjoy print books, which means the children's library should provide access to both print and digital books for children of all ages. Lower-income families have less access to digital tablets (such as iPads) at home and provide fewer opportunities for their

Text continues on page 80

Digital Media with Children: A Library Educator Perspective from Marianne Martens

H aving worked in the children's publishing industry and as a children's book translator and children's librarian, library and information science professor Marianne Martens has a well-informed, global view of children's literature, librarianship, and digital media. In her librarian preparation courses at Kent State University (Ohio), Marianne examines the intersection of print and digital media in the lives of contemporary children and adolescents, challenging librarians to explore hard questions about the role of new digital media and books in library collections and programs. She believes that media mentorship is a new and evolving role for contemporary children's librarians. As more digital formats permeate society, it is important for librarians to be media mentors when parents can't give the digital literacy help their children need. Marianne notes, "librarians need the necessary skills to provide access to the digital content and serve as digital curators of new media, helping parents select the best apps for their children. They have to be on the cutting edge of new technology."

She also suggests that children's librarians be conscious of the role that digital media can play in the lives of children, understand why digital literacy skills are important as well as how to incorporate them into library programming, and have the ability to model purposeful use of digital media and children's books in the library. "I agree with thinkers like Lisa Guernsey and Cen Campbell that co-viewing is important," Marianne remarks. "Parents should be alongside their children as they explore digital apps. When I was a child our TV was controlled—regulated and doled out. The same should go for apps today. As children get older, parents want to be sure that they are reading on their digital devices and not only surfing the web for fun."

Marianne also acknowledges the tension among children's librarians concerning the role of digital media in the library and the perceived threat that apps and e-books will replace physical books. She sees apps as a complementary new form of media, but does not perceive them eliminating books in the library, particularly as digital tablets are significantly more expensive to replace than books. Marianne explains that digital notebooks should certainly have a place in the children's library but there also needs to be plenty of materials that can go home with families as well.

However, she does note advantages of digital media over print materials. "As much as I love apps, I love print books too. I don't think the print book is a bad—dead—thing," Marianne asserts. "Digital formats can take readers beyond the confines of the print format. A nonfiction app such as *Bats! Furry Flyers of the Night* allows kids to experience the bats' eye view, has pictures of bats, allows viewers to see skeletal structures, and includes bat sounds. With a print book on bats, the reader could lift a flap and see skeletal structure, but the multimedia component with the app allows for many more possibilities. In this particular case the app could be better than a print book." On the other hand, she acknowledges that some apps can serve a complementary role to printed books. Marianne observes that, "Mo Willems's *Don't Let the Pigeon Run This App!* is different from *Don't Let Pigeon Drive the Bus*. The app allows kids to see and hear Mo Willems, draw their own version of Pigeon's story, and record their voice. In this case, the app supplements and extends the book. I think it is a different thing. With nonfiction apps you can enrich and extend, and with fiction apps you can go in completely different directions."

On the flip side, print materials have certain advantages over digital media. It is important to keep in mind considerations such as the origination of content and issues surrounding ownership and privacy. Some books start out in a print format and then move to a digital version without changes. Marianne remarks, "This just doesn't work. You have a picture book being shoved into a new platform without modifications. If you think back to the 1990s, there was an explosion of multicultural books and publishers were scrambling to meet market demands. Some publishers that wanted a Spanish-language version of a book would strip the English books of their text and dump Spanish text in place of it. These looked horrible since they weren't native Spanish-language books. The same can be said for digital books and apps that start out in a print format and go digital without adjustments for the new platform." Without the necessary modifications, the app can create a frustrating experience for children.

Privacy can also be a concern when using an e-book or other type of digital media. Marianne cautions, "When a child reads an e-book on a Kindle, Amazon is taking down market information. Similarly when using particular apps on an iPad, information is being collected and sent back to the producer of the app. This is a way of studying user interaction with books in digital format. It is a kind of Big Brother creepy surveillance that is endemic to the digital format." Another concern with digital media is ownership. Do you really own a digital book the same way you own a print book? Marianne reminds us that Amazon can erase books off a Kindle after they are purchased. Also, as platforms evolve, digital devices become obsolete and there is no way to keep a digital book forever. Digital books can't be lent to friends the same way print books are

Figure 4.5 continues on page 80

shared. To share a digital book, users have to lend the entire platform or device. Similarly, batteries may die on devices or limits may be placed on the use of digital devices while flying. Print books do not have the same restrictions, offering readers more mobility.

On a final note, Marianne emphasizes the ability of apps to promote digital literacy and bridge linguistically diverse cultures. With an app, users can switch the language of the text and audio to either mirror their home language or to foster learning a new language. This feature works

Text continued from page 77

children to use educational and creative apps. To help bridge the digital divide, children's librarians can provide access to tablet and educational/creative apps and facilitate learning opportunities for children and their families to learn how to use the digital media together. Moreover, children's librarians can learn how to select, evaluate, and use digital media such as apps in the children's library. Simon and Nemeth (2012) note, "It's about the choices you make: your curriculum, your practice, and how you use *whatever* [emphasis in orig.] materials you plan for children to explore and learn from—not whether or not the material is digital. Rejecting technology for your program because it *can be* [emphasis in orig.] used inappropriately or because *some* [emphasis in orig.] applications are inappropriate is like throwing out the baby with the bathwater!" (p. 19). As the aforementioned statistics show, both the baby and the bathwater are here to stay. It's time for librarians to provide the bubbles!

References

American Academy of Pediatrics, Council on Communications and Media. "Children, Adolescents, and the Media." *Pediatrics* 132, no. 5 (November 1, 2013): 958–961.

Bryant, Alison (January 2014). *What a Difference a Year Makes: Kids and E-Reading Trends 2012–13*. Wilmington, DE: PlayCollective LLC and Digital Book World. Accessed January 21, 2014, at http://store. digitalbookworld.com/what-difference-a-year-makes-childrens-report-t3592.

Campaign for a Commercial-Free Childhood, Alliance for Childhood, and Teachers Resisting Unhealthy Children's Entertainment. (October 2012). Facing the Screen Dilemma:

toward bridging cultures, but Marianne believes more multicultural and global literature should be available in digital formats. She laments, "I think it is alarming that most multicultural books aren't available in digital formats." It is alarming indeed, but a plague that has befallen print children's books for decades. Hopefully, as our nation diversifies and new digital media appear so will the quantity and quality of multicultural digital content.

Figure 4.5: Digital Media with Children: A Library Educator Perspective from Marianne Martens

Young Children, Technology and Early Education. Boston, MA: Campaign for a Commercial-Free Childhood; New York, NY: Alliance for Childhood. Accessed March 1, 2014, at http://www.commercialfreechildhood.org/sites/default/files/facingthescreendilemma.pdf.

Common Sense Media. (Fall 2013). *Zero to Eight: Children's Media Use in America 2013*. New York: Common Sense Media. Accessed December 31, 2013, at http://www.commonsensemedia.org/research/zero-to-eight-childrens-media-use-in-america-2013.

Guernsey, Lisa, Michael Levine, Cynthia Chiong, and Maggie Severns. (2012). *Pioneering Literacy in the Digital Wild West: Empowering Parents and Educators: A Primer for Communities*. New York: The Joan Ganz Cooney Center at Sesame Workshop and New America Foundation, 2012. Accessed December 30, 2013, at http://gradelevelreading.net/wp-content/uploads/2012/12/GLR_TechnologyGuide_final.pdf.

Hansen, Genesis. (December 13, 2013). Response to "The Baby and the Bathwater: A Nuanced Message About Screen Time." *The Digital Media Diet*. Accessed December 18, 2013, at http://digitalmediadiet.com/wp-trackback.php?p=3036.

Kleckner, Kathy. (June 14, 2013). "The Screen Free Story Time Is the Best Story Time." *ALSC Blog*. Accessed February 22, 2014, at http://www.alsc.ala.org/blog/2013/06/the-screen-free-story-time-is-the-best-story-time/.

Kluver, Carisa. (June 22, 2013). "Do Screens Belong in Library Storytimes for Young Children? Response to ALSC Blog." *The Digital Media*

Diet. Accessed February 22, 2014, at http://digitalmediadiet.
com/?p=2714#sthash.ezX3PEqH.dpuf.

Korat, Ofra, and Adina Shamir. "Electronic Books Versus Adult Readers:
Effects on Children's Emergent Literacy as a Function of Social
Class." *Journal of Computer Assisted Learning* 23, no. 3 (2007):
248–259.

National Association for the Education of Young Children and the Fred
Rogers Center for Early Learning and Children's Media. (January
2012). *Technology and Interactive Media as Tools in Early Childhood
Programs Serving Children from Birth Through Age 8.* Joint
position statement. Washington, DC: NAEYC; Latrobe, PA: Fred
Rogers Center for Early Learning and Children's Media. Accessed
December 28, 2013, at http://www.naeyc.org/content/technology-
and-young-children.

Nemeth, Karen N., and Cen Campbell. "Getting to Know the New
Children's Librarian." *Teaching Young Children* 7, no. 2 (2013):
27–28.

Parrott, Kiera. (November 14, 2011). "Circulating iPads in the Children's
Library." *ALSC Blog.* Accessed January 1, 2014, at http://www.alsc.
ala.org/blog/2011/11/circulating-ipads-in-the-childrens-library/ .

Roskos, Kathleen, Karen Burstein, Yi Shang, and Emily Gray. "Young
Children's Engagement with E-Books at School: Does Device
Matter?" *SAGE Open* 4, no. 1 (2014): 1–9.

Scholastic. (January 2013). *Kids and Family Reading Report.* 4th ed.
Accessed December 31, 2013, at http://mediaroom.scholastic.com/
files/kfrr2013-noappendix.pdf.

Simon, Fran, and Karen Nemeth. *Digital Decisions: Choosing the Right
Technology Tools for Early Childhood Education.* Lewisville, NC:
Gryphon House, 2012.

Steiner-Adair, Catherine, and Teresa H. Barker. *The Big Disconnect:
Protecting Childhood and Family Relationships in the Digital Age.*
New York: Harper, 2013.

III

Putting It All Together

◊ Chapter 5

Current Cultural and Digital Literacy Programs for Children

Cultural literacy programs are library programs that celebrate diverse cultures and the contributions of members from various cultural groups, provide opportunities for people from diverse cultural backgrounds to make cross-cultural/intercultural connections, and foster the development and reinforcement of cultural competence among librarians, caregivers, and children. If children and families participate in cultural literacy programs then the likelihood of them eventually developing cultural competence is higher than for those who do not participate in such library programs.

Within in the past twenty years, numerous dynamic library and literacy programs have been developed that provide opportunities for children and families to make intercultural connections and celebrate global literature for children. While most of these programs do not currently have a component that promotes digital literacy or includes the use of new digital media, modifications can be made to extend the reach of these programs to attract digital natives. This chapter highlights these cultural literacy programs and provides suggestions for integrating relevant digital media. It also explores specific high-quality digital library program models that either promote cultural competence or could be modified to include culturally diverse materials.

Examples of Cultural Literacy Programs

Día: Children's Day/Book Day

One of the oldest programs celebrating cultural literacy is El día de los niños/ El día de los libros or Children's Day/Book Day (Día for short), established almost twenty years ago in 1996 by Latina children's author, educator, and poet Pat Mora. Combining elements of the international celebration Day of the Child with the celebration of reading enjoyment (Bookjoy), Día honors children and reading, promotes bilingual and multilingual literacy, highlights multicultural and global children's literature, and fosters global understanding among children and their families. Public and school libraries around the nation have adopted the celebration, and each year REFORMA (the National Association to Promote Library and Information Services to Latinos and the Spanish-Speaking) presents the Mora Award for exemplary Día programs. For several years the Association for Library Service to Children (ALSC), in partnership with Dollar General, has also awarded mini-grants to help libraries initiate Día programming or start a Día Family Book Club. From an all-out Díapalooza to daily celebrations of Día, there are many innovative ways that libraries can celebrate Día and promote cultural competence throughout the year.

With its focus on bringing global citizens together, building community, and celebrating diverse languages and cultures, Día helps to build what global literacy pioneer Jella Lepman (1964) calls "bridges of understanding," where books and literacy programs are used as the vehicle for helping children and families cultivate respect and understanding for each other. As a daily commitment to link children from all cultural and linguistic backgrounds to books, Día also builds bridges of bookjoy. Founder Pat Mora remarks, "Together, cada día, every day, we're building the bridge to bookjoy" (2011, p. 8). Día is both a daily celebration of culture and a yearly culminating fiesta of books and reading on April 30th.

Librarians can also use the celebration to promote digital literacy. By getting digital with Día, libraries have an opportunity to connect digital natives with high-quality multicultural digital media, global children's books, and exciting cultural literacy programming. In Día programming for early school-age children, a librarian might read books relating to culturally specific music/musicians or music around the world and provide opportunities for children to use digital apps to explore the style of music addressed or to create their own songs. For example, a program might include the book *Tito*

Puente, Mambo King/Tito Puente, Rey del Mambo by Monica Brown and Rafael López, which showcases the musical style of musician Tito Puente, along with the book *Drummer Boy of John John* by Mark Greenwood and Frané Lessac, which follows a boy from Trinidad as he makes music out of everyday junk in preparation for Carnival. After hearing the stories read and listening to samples of Puente's music as well as Carnival music, children could engage in creative play with SPYE Studio's digital app *Drum Circle Kids,* where children are introduced to the American Trap Set, Caribbean Steel Pan, Chinese Drum, Cuban Conga, West African Djembe, and other drums. Librarians could also encourage children to create their own digital drum circle jam sessions. As a further extension, librarians could discuss drum circles, read a book about drum circles in Cuba such as *Drum, Chavi, Drum!/¡Toca, Chavi, toca!* by Mayra Lazara Dole and Tonel, and have children use drums to participate in a live drum circle in the story room of the library. Through this program, children would learn about drumming music from around the world, strengthening their musical literacy skills, honing digital literacy skills as they use the app, and making cross-cultural connections and celebrating bookjoy through the various culturally diverse books being shared.

Another example of getting digital with Día would include librarians sharing the book *Book Fiesta! Celebrate Children's Day/Book Day; Celebremos El día de los ninos/El día de los líbros* by Pat Mora and Rafael López and talking about the actual meaning of the Día celebration. Children could listen to an interview with both the author and illustrator from the ¡Colorín Colorado! website (http://www.colorincolorado.org/calendar/celebrations/dia/). The official Día song from Pat Mora's webpage could be displayed and played using an iPad and an LCD projector and screen, and then children could use Olivier Romanetti's *Music4Kids* app to create their own musical score. As in the other digital Día program, children are honing their musical, digital, and cultural literacy skills in the library.

Planning a Día event might seem like a daunting task for librarians, but there are numerous resources available to assist in the planning, development, promotion, execution, and evaluation of Día programs. These resources include lists of recommended global children's books celebrating many cultures, suggested finger rhymes and songs, librarian-approved hands-on craft activities, thematic storytime ideas, year-long program suggestions, and much more. See Figure 5.1 for an extensive list of resources.

Resources for Planning Día Programs

Official Día Website—This extensive website contains a plethora of resources relating to planning and promoting Día programs as well as links to multicultural and bilingual booklists, book club ideas, a year-long planning guide, grant information, and free publisher posters celebrating Día. http://dia.ala.org/

Día de los Niños/Día de los Libros: A Celebration of Childhood and Bilingual Literacy—Created by the California State Library and sponsored by a grant from the Institute of Museum and Library Services, this comprehensive website contains a Día planning checklist, downloadable customizable graphics, bookmarks, press releases, and activity suggestions. http://www.diacalifornia.org/

Dígame un cuento/Tell Me a Story: Bilingual Library Programs for Children and Families—Created by the Texas State Library and Archives Commission, this online manual recommends bilingual storyhour programs for Latino children and their families. Librarians can use this resource to plan activities for Día that celebrate Latino cultures. http://www.tsl.state.tx.us/ld/pubs/bilingual/index.html

El Día de los Niños/El Día de los Libros: A Celebration of Childhood and Bilingual Literacy—Created by the Texas State Library and Archives Commission, this website contains a variety of information related to planning a Día celebration including fingerplays, downloadable Spanish/English rhymes and songs, suggested activities, bookmarks, a bibliography of recommended bilingual books, and a list of helpful resources. http://www.tsl.state.tx.us/ld/projects/ninos/index.html

El dia de los Niños/El dia de los libros (Day of the Child/Day of the Book) Toolkit—A 100-page online document that describes booktalks, author visits, storytelling, and other programming ideas that can be used to celebrate Día on April 30th and throughout the entire year. http://www.texasdia.org/toolkit.html

El día de los niños/El día de los libros—This webpage, part of ¡Colorín Colorado!'s dynamic website celebrating multicultural and bilingual children's literature and literacy, includes Día video interviews with many

Latina children's book creators, activities, a Día e-card, and lists of recommended multicultural children's books. http://www. colorincolorado.org/calendar/ celebrations/dia

Día: El día de los niños/El día de los libros—This fantastic website includes information on the history of Día, the Día song, Pat Mora's Día picture book *Book Fiesta,* Pat Mora's *Children's Days, Book Days: Planning for a Día Year,* information on how to say Día in 15 languages, and multiple resources and articles about the celebration. http://www. patmora.com/whats-dia and http://www.patmora.com/dia-planning-booklet/

"The Spirit of Día: Celebrating Cuentos Every Day"—Irania Macias Patterson and Jamie Campbell Naidoo. In J. C. Naidoo (ed.), *Celebrating Cuentos: Promoting Latino Children's Literature and Literacy in Classrooms and Libraries* (pp. 201–212). Santa Barbara, CA: Libraries Unlimited, 2010.

Celebrating Culture, Reading, and Family Literacy @ the Library with the Latino Reading and Literacy Programs El día de los niños/El día de los libros (Día) and Noche de Cuentos—Jamie Campbell Naidoo, Patricia Montiel-Overall, Lucia Gonzalez, Oralia Garza de Cortés, and Irania Macias Patterson. 2010 IFLA Conference Proceedings. http://conference.ifla.org/past/2010/133-naidoo-en.pdf.

El día de los niños/El día de los libros: Building a Culture of Literacy in Your Community Through Día—Jeanette Larson. Chicago: American Library Association, 2011.

Figure 5.1: Resources for Planning Día Programs

American Library Association Family Literacy Focus Programs

In January 2010 the American Library Association (ALA), under the direction of ALA 2009–2010 President Dr. Camila Alire, launched the Family Literacy Focus (FLF) initiative in conjunction with ALA's five Ethnic Caucuses. The purpose of FLF is to motivate families in ethnically diverse communities to engage in literacy activities such as reading, writing, and storytelling. Each of the Ethnic Caucuses received funds to design innovative, replicable family literacy library programs. The end products of the funding ranged from websites and brochures to manuals and toolkits to bibliographies and mini-grants to support pilot FLF programs in librar ies across the nation. Collectively, the Ethnic Caucuses—the American Indian Library Association (AILA), the Asian Pacific American Librarians Association (APALA), the Black Caucus of the American Library Association (BCALA), the Chinese American Librarians Association (CALA), and REFORMA (the National Association to Promote Library and Information Services to Latinos and the Spanish-Speaking)—developed four unique types of programs. These cultural literacy programs promote understanding of diverse cultural groups and hold potential for also engaging digital natives as they further develop their digital literacy skills. The subsequent subsections outline the four programs designed by the ethnic affiliates.

Talk Story: Sharing Stories, Sharing Culture

Developed through a partnership of AILA and APALA, Talk Story: Sharing Stories, Sharing Culture is a cultural literacy program celebrating Asian Pacific American (APA) and American Indian/Alaska Native (AIAN) cultures through books, storytelling, and creative activities. According to program developers, "*talk story* is a Hawaiian term referring to an informal style of conversation where a person shares a story while others corroborate or add to it as it is being told" (American Library Association, 2014, par. 17). The purpose of Talk Story is to support family literacy and promote cultural literacy by scaffolding opportunities for both caregivers and children to work together to strengthen literacy skills and learn through high-quality books and dynamic library programs about the contributions that APA and AIAN cultures have made to society. Generally a Talk Story program includes group readings of rich children's literature about various aspects of the APA and AIAN cultures, followed by informal storytelling and crafts that serve as extensions to further develop cultural understanding. While the program can be used during Asian American and Asian Pacific Islander Heritage Month and Native American Heritage Month, it easily lends itself to year-round celebrations and children's programming that promote positive ethnic identity development of APA and AIAN children and open doors to understanding for children from other cultures. Talk Story's extensive website includes customizable promotional materials (flyers, brochures, and posters), a storytime database chock full of thematic programming, selection criteria for choosing books with APA and AIAN themes, recommended bibliographies of children's books, and an 81-page program toolkit. This Talk Story toolkit includes programming ideas, templates, family literacy tips, and practical suggestions for making community connections. Since the inception of the program, Toyota Financial Services has continuously provided financial support for mini-grants to help libraries successfully deliver Talk Story programs.

Librarians interested in incorporating digital media into a Talk Story program might consider an app such as Isreal Shortman's *Navajo Toddler*, which teaches Navajo language learners basic words for numbers, food, animals, colors, and so forth. During a storytime, this app could be shared with children and parents by connecting a digital tablet to the LCD projector and displaying the various Navajo words on a large screen. Books such as *Colors of the Navajo* by Emily Abbink and Janice Porter or Beverly Blacksheep's Baby Learns series could be read aloud and then the librarian or caregivers could connect to the storytelling theme of Talk Story by sharing versions of any number of the Navajo coyote tales. The significance of language and oral tradition to Navajo culture could also be explored.

A Talk Story program focused on Filipino culture could include reading the picture book *Cora Cooks Pancit* by Dorina Gilmore and Kristi Valiant, either in print format or using the iPad and LCD projector to explore the TumbleBooks version of the story, and accompanying the book with Filipino children's book publisher Adarna House's *A Day in the Market* picture book app, based on the Philippine National Children's Book Award-winning picture book *Araw sa Palengke* by May Tobias-Papa and Isabel Roxas. This award-winning, beautifully illustrated, interactive app is available in Filipino or English and includes activities and games. As both *A Day in the Market* and *Cora Cooks Pancit* focus on cooking, a hands-on activity might include cooking a simple Filipino dish. To further immerse children and families in Filipino culture, librarians might include Filipino rhymes and songs either from a web source such as Mama Lisa's World Kids Songs and Rhymes from the Philippines (http://www.mamalisa.com/?t=ec&p=981&c=150) or one of the children's apps of Filipino children's songs. The book *Filipino Celebrations: A Treasury of Feasts and Festivals* by Liana Romulo and Corazon Dandan-Albano also includes a wealth of background information on Filipino culture along with crafts and games that might be used for hands-on crafts in lieu of cooking. Finally, to connect with the storytelling theme of Talk Story, caregivers or the librarian can share Filipino stories such as those found in Liana Romulo and Joanne de Leon's *Filipino Children's Favorite Stories*. Additional information can be found at http://talkstorytogether.org/.

Reading Is Grand! Celebrating Grand-Families @ Your Library

Created by the Black Caucus of the American Library Association, Reading Is Grand! Celebrating-Grand-Families @ Your Library is a family literacy program focusing on the grandparent-grandchild relationship, particularly instances where grandparents are the primary caregivers. Within the African American community these *grand-families* are becoming more common, with grandparents raising and educating their grandchildren. The Reading Is Grand program includes three major components: (1) celebrating the important role of grandparents in the lives of children, (2) offering outreach to grandparent caregivers, and (3) promoting literacy through shared oral and written stories. According to the program's website, grandparents share their wisdom and rich life experiences with grandchildren as a way to help the younger generation learn cultural values necessary for becoming active members in our global society. With this in mind, the Reading Is Grand program offers several suggestions for how grandparents can promote literacy with their grandchildren by sharing oral stories and memories, reading culturally responsive literature, and visiting the library. One of these suggestions includes asking grandparents to share childhood stories with their grandchildren, encouraging children to write down and illustrate these stories, and then reading the story together. Grandparents are also prompted to visit the library to find nonfiction children's titles reflecting something from their own childhoods and then reading these books with their grandchildren. Additionally, the program places a strong emphasis on shared reading enjoyment through books celebrating the lives of grandparents. To this end, the program website provides an example of a successful Reading Is Grand library program, promotional materials, and a bibliography of recommended African American children's and young adult books that celebrate family diversity in the form of either extended families or those honoring grandparents. While not as extensive as the Talk

Story website, Reading Is Grand's major strength is its valuable list of often overlooked titles that strongly support grand-family literacy. Librarians can modify their version of the program to focus on global grandparents or other aspects of the African American culture.

An example of a Reading Is Grand digital children's program for elementary children using the idea of global grandparents could include sharing the books *When I Am Old with You* by Angela Johnson and David Soman and *Grandma's Chocolate/El Chocolate de Abuelita* by Mara Price and Lisa Fields, which examine the relationships between children and grandparents who are African American and Latino respectively. After these stories are read aloud, grandparents and children could explore an interactive book and creative app such as Green Label's *My Grandma Reads Me Books,* which follows a young Chinese girl as she reads stories to her illiterate grandmother each night before bedtime and eventually teaches her elder to read. The app includes the ability for children to paint a picture for their grandparent or even record their own story! Librarians could share the story using a tablet and projector and then allow children and grandparents to play with the app on individual tablets, recording their voices and telling stories. If a children's librarian wanted to spark a discussion where grandparents share their memories of significant historical events with grandchildren, then she could read the book *The Day Gogo Went to Vote* by Elinor Batezat Sisulu and Sharon Wilson, which follows a South African grandmother as she votes the first time after the end of apartheid. Grandparents and children could then dive into the collection to find books representing significant historical moments from their own pasts. A final extension could be a passive programming station where grandparents and grandchildren use a storytelling app to record and share special family stories. For more information on Reading Is Grand, consult the program website: bcalareadingisgrand.weebly.com.

Dai Dai Xiang Chuan: Bridging Generations, a Bag at a Time

Designed by the Chinese American Librarians Association, the cultural and family literacy program Dai Dai Xiang Chuan: Bridging Generations, a Bag at a Time improves "intergenerational literacy, cultural awareness, and life skills for immigrant families and families with adopted children from China and Chinese speaking countries" (American Library Association, 2014, par. 6). Dai Dai Xiang Chuan is a pun on the words "generation" and "bags," which are pronounced the same in Chinese but written differently. Essentially the program name means to share and pass on knowledge from one generation to the next. The goal of Dai Dai Xiang Chuan is to use storytelling, technology, movement, and shared reading to bridge the divergent experiences of extended family members and create lasting family literacy encounters that celebrate Chinese and Chinese American culture. Libraries participating in the program create bilingual Chinese/English literacy bags to use during programming and to circulate in the community. These bags include books, online resources, DVDs, flash cards, recipes, and craft ideas and materials that focus on themes relating to Chinese cultural celebrations and activities.

The Dai Dai Xiang Chuan program website (http://daidai.cala-web. org/) contains information on mini-grants to support programming and includes examples of successful programs in public libraries across the United States. Numerous professional resources are included to help librarians in program planning. These include an extensive bibliography of articles relating to family literacy and online links to Chinese recipes, family literacy programs focusing on Chinese culture, general family literacy programs in the United States and Canada, and information on creating literacy bags.

To extend the program to include digital literacy, librarians could use an interactive app such as Mark Animation's *Learn with Miaomiao: Chinese* to teach basic oral and written Chinese characters and words through games and creative play. The app could be demonstrated using the digital tablet, LCD projector, and screen, and then families could play with the app using personal or library tablets. The bilingual Chinese/English website 5QChannel includes games, e-books, and apps that teach English to Chinese-speaking children and Chinese to English-speaking children. While some of the content contains cultural stereotypes in the images, librarians can find useful content to make available on stand-alone computers or wireless digital tablets in the children's department.

Another option would be to explore various traditional elements of Chinese culture relating to Chinese New Year through the app *Magikid Nian* by Magikid. Nian in the title of the app comes from a traditional Chinese folktale about a monster/dragon that scared a village before Chinese New Year. The interactive app includes games, culturally appropriate songs, and an option for children and intergenerational family members to record their own stories about Chinese New Year. Particularly appealing about the app is the inclusion of children from around the world, reinforcing the idea that the holiday is celebrating globally. *Magikid Nian* could supplement a storytime on Chinese culture that includes the books *A New Year's Reunion: A Chinese Story* by Yu Li-Qiong and Zhu Cheng-Liang and *Bringing in the New Year* by Grace Lin. After reading the stories, a librarian could introduce songs from the app and encourage families to write down their own stories about Chinese New Year or a favorite family memory. These could then be recorded using a storytelling app or the storytelling feature of *Magikid Nian*. The only drawback to the app is that users must complete various tasks or games before getting to the songs. A librarian would need to advance to a song stage before being able to use it in storytime. The storybook app by Rye Books entitled *The Beast Nian* could also be shared with attendees to give more information about Nian. If a librarian didn't want to focus on Chinese New Year, other books by Grace Lin could easily be substituted.

Noche de Cuentos: Night of Stories

Produced by REFORMA (the National Association to Promote Library and Information Services to Latinos and the Spanish-Speaking), Noche de Cuentos is a family and cultural literacy program that celebrates the power and potential for storytelling to maintain cultural heritage within the Latino community. The program highlights the importance of literacy in the United States and provides an avenue for Latino families to learn more about the programs, services, and collections offered by libraries. Noche de Cuentos also promotes oral and cultural literacy by focusing on the rich oral stories from Latino cultures. Libraries participating in the program develop opportunities for intergenerational sharing of oral and written stories. This can be accomplished through grandparents sharing oral stories and children recording them to create digital stories or writing them down to create personalized story books. Cultural stories and songs can capture the experiences of their families, communities, and native countries.

While the program focuses on Latino culture, it can be extended to represent other cultural groups. The Noche de Cuentos website (http://nochedecuentos.org/) contains numerous resources to assist librarians in designing their own Night of Stories. Included on the website are bibliographies of storytelling resources, recommended sources of Latino children's stories for retelling, marketing materials, and information about minigrants to fund programming.

Going digital with Noche de Cuentos can be accomplished through the inclusion of web resources and digital apps relating to Latino culture, literature, songs, storytelling, and more. A librarian might read the book *My Abuelita* by Tony Johnston and Yuyi Morales and show children the TumbleBook version of *I Love Saturdays y Domingos* by Alma Flor Ada and Elivia Savadier using the digital tablet. Both books are about a child's relationship with his/her grandparents, and the first book also introduces the idea of storytelling. A storytelling app, such as Go and Create's *I Tell a Story* or Haywoodsoft's *Story Patch,* could then be used to help children and intergenerational family members record their own stories. The children's stories might be a favorite memory of their grandparent or a favorite story their grandparent told them. Another example of digital media in a Noche de Cuentos program would be the inclusion of Lunave Multimedio's *Loteria* gaming app. A librarian could read the book *Playing Loteria/El juego de la loteria* by Rene Colato Laínez and Jill Arena, which is about a young boy playing the loteria game with his grandmother, and then display the Loteria gaming app on a large screen using the LCD projector and digital tablet. Families could play the game together while waiting to use library equipment (video camera, photo editing software, etc.) to create digital stories about favorite family traditions or games. Digital stories could then be shared with everyone.

Bridging Cultures: Muslim Journeys

Supported by the National Endowment for the Humanities in collaboration with the American Library Association's Public Program Office, Bridging Cultures: Muslim Journeys is a literary and literacy initiative supporting explorations into the Muslim cultures and includes the Bookshelf and Let's Talk About It program discussion series (http://bridgingcultures.neh.gov/muslimjourneys/ and http://www.programminglibrarian.org/muslimjourneys/ltai/mj-ltai.html). The Muslim Journeys website, developed by the Ali Vural Ak Center for Global Islamic Studies at George Mason University, provides recommended titles for adults and programming suggestions. Although the program was not developed with children in mind, the basic goals of the initiative and features of the Let's Talk About It discussion series can be adapted for use with families and children. According to the Muslim Journey's ALA website, the program "seeks to introduce readers to some new and diverse perspectives on the people, places, histories, beliefs, practices, and cultures of Muslims in the United States and around the world. The collection has been organized around five themes, including American Stories, Connected Histories, Literary Reflections, Pathways of Faith and Points of View" (American Library Association Muslim Journeys, 2013, par. 3). Children's librarians could select a variety of fiction and nonfiction books about Muslim cultures and arrange them around the Muslim Journey's five themes. Book discussion programs could be developed around these books as well as storytime programs with hands-on activities, crafts, songs, and digital resources. Recommended books could be chosen from the Association for Library Service to Children's (ALSC's) Books on Islam for Children and Teens list (http://www.ala.org/alsc/com-pubs/booklists/islambooks).

Numerous high-quality children's digital apps are available on Muslim topics and could be used in digital storytimes to promote cultural literacy. For young children, a librarian could read aloud the picture books *Golden Domes and Silver Lanterns: A Muslim Book of Colors* by Hena Khan and Mehrdokht Amini and *Night of the Moon: A Muslim Holiday Story* by Hena Khan and Julie Paschkis. Afterward, he or she could share the picture book and puzzle app *Kids of the Ummah: Exploring the Global Muslim Community* by Magnicode and Peter Gould, which explores the great diversity within the Muslim culture. An activity and party-planning guide to support the app is available at http://www.kidsoftheummah.com/. Other children's apps about the Muslim culture can be found on the Muslim Parents Network's blog: http://muslimparentsnetwork.org/top-islamic-apps-for-you-kids-itunes-andriod/. Additional information about the Muslim Journeys initiative is available on the NEH Muslim Journeys website (http://bridgingcultures.neh.gov/muslimjourneys/) and the ALA Muslim Journeys website (http://www.programminglibrarian.org/muslim-journeys/).

Sister Libraries Program

Developed by the Libraries for Children and Young Adults Section of the International Federation of Library Associations and Institutions (IFLA), the Sister Libraries Program provides an avenue for children's libraries to develop global partnerships, collaborate, and develop joint literacy programs promoting global children's and young adult literature. According to the program's website and brochure, children's librarians participating in the Sister Libraries Program can work with children's librarians in other countries to share ideas on library programming and information-related collection development and best practices. In addition, librarians in Sister Libraries can exchange photos of library programs and environment, create opportunities for virtual visits and interviews, design cross-cultural reading clubs or book discussions where children read the same book and discuss or explore books about/from the other country, and develop displays about the sister library's community, city, state/province, region, and country.

As one of the goals of the Sister Libraries Program is to promote cross-cultural connections, librarians might pair the picture book *Same, Same But Different* by Jenny Sue Kostecki-Shaw with the picture-book app *Up and Down* by Mr. Garamond. In both instances, two boys from two very different countries examine the numerous ways in which they are different but the same. This would be a great way to introduce children and families to the idea of communicating with children in other countries and the idea of the Sister Libraries Program. Under the supervision of the children's librarians, children can use ePals Global Community (www.ep-als.com) to connect with other children around the world and make global connections around literature. Features allow children to publish their own stories and have their own mock book awards and literature discussions. Of particular relevance to the Sister Libraries Program is the ability to connect with classrooms of other students in the same city or region as the children in the Sister Library.

Another way in which children's librarians can incorporate digital apps into a Sister Libraries Program is to share apps between the two libraries and have children explore and evaluate the apps from different cultural perspectives. Children could also investigate interactive book or educational apps that either teach about the culture of the Sister Library or represent high-quality apps from the country. Global children's apps that explore universal themes and experiences through literature, such as *Being Global* by SachManya and Little Pickle Press, could be used to spark children's creativity to design their own digital stories using storytelling apps. More information about the Sister Libraries Program, including examples of successful activities and partnerships, can be found on the Sister Libraries blog: http://sisterlibraries.wordpress.com/.

International Children's Book Day and World Read Aloud Day

Two children's literary and literacy programs celebrate global children's literature, reading and cultural literacy, and reading enjoyment. These programs highlight high-quality books and book creators from various countries and provide philanthropic opportunities to support reading literacy efforts around the world. Each year since 1967 on or around April 2nd, International Children's Book Day (ICBD) celebrates Bookjoy and the prominent work of children's book creators. A National Section of the International Board on Books for Young People (IBBY) is selected as the international sponsor, choosing a theme and a prominent children's author from the country to write a message to the children of the world and a well-known illustrator to create an ICBD poster. Additional information is available at http://www.ibby.org.

World Read Aloud Day is a literacy and philanthropic program developed by LitWorld, a non-profit organization that fosters resilience, hope, and joy through the power of story. Each year on the first Wednesday in March, World Read Aloud Day celebrates global literacy and the potential of storytelling, and reading aloud in the lives of children. Children, librarians, educators, and caregivers around the globe gather to share stories and create a community that advocates for every child's right to a safe, high-quality education and access to books and technology. Participants can share stories virtually via Skype or digital storytelling or face-to-face. In addition, there is an opportunity to participate in fundraisers providing reading materials and educational opportunities to children who might not otherwise have these luxuries. More information on World Read Aloud Day is available at http://litworld.org/worldreadaloudday.

Incorporating digital global children's literature into International Children's Book Day and World Read Aloud Day is easy with digital apps and other types of digital media. For free access to global e-books, librarians can visit the International Children's Digital Library (http://en.childrenslibrary.org/), which houses more than 4,500 children's picture books and novels in 61 languages. These books can be displayed using an LCD projector and shared in library programs. Book apps featuring stories from or about specific countries can be used in both ICBD and World Read Aloud Day celebrations. *One Globe Kids: Children's Stories from Around the World,* created by Round by Design, is a multilingual app introducing children to informational stories about real children living around the world. Librarians can use this app in a cultural literacy program to explore the lives of global children and then encourage children and families to dive into the collection for other fiction and nonfiction titles representing the cultures of the children depicted in the app.

Examples of Digital Library Programs for Children

The aforementioned examples demonstrate dynamic library programs and celebrations that promote cultural competence and intercultural connections among children and their families. For the most part, none of these programs have a particular element that incorporates digital media (although digital media can easily be included in any of them). While profiles of vibrant digital storytimes and children's programs promoting cultural competence would be a wonderful way to showcase the potential of new digital media in the library, very few exist because of the timely nature of the topic! This section highlights a program in rural Maine that uses iPads to reach migrant Latino children and families, and a pilot program from the U.S. Department of Education that uses a well-known cartoon character to teach English to Spanish-speaking Latino children. The other programs that we describe in this section are outstanding samples of digital story-time models. Hopefully as more multicultural apps and other digital media become available, creative children's librarians will be able to use these examples for inspirations for their own digital storytimes that encourage cultural competence.

Comienza en Casa/It Starts at Home

Started in spring 2012, Comienza en Casa/It Starts at Home is a digital literacy program developed by the Maine Migrant Education Program and the nonprofit organization Mano en Mano/Hand in Hand. Using hands-on activities, children's books, iPad apps, and family discussion, the goal of the program is to facilitate school readiness and literacy skills for young children (preschool and kindergarten) who have limited English proficiency. The program includes the following components: read, play, create, off-screen, family focus, and free play.

- Read: Children and parents read a Spanish translation of an English book from the curriculum focusing on such topics as colors, counting, nature, and relationships. Depending on the age and proficiency of the child, the parent either reads the book to the child or the child reads the book to a sibling/parent. Reading comprehension questions or prompts are provided for the family to explore.

- Play (structured): The parent and child explore an educational app together with the child leading and parent assisting. These apps (*My Very First App, Write My Name*, etc.) are basic, available in English or Spanish, and expand upon the topic/concept introduced in the children's book. Suggested topics and questions to answer are provided.

- Create: Families explore an interactive creating app (*Doodlecast* and *Story Kit,* for example) with the child leading and parent assisting. Prompting questions that provide scaffolding of previously introduced concepts are given along with suggested in-app activities for the child to complete.

◊ Offscreen: Children, assisted by parents, engage in several hands-on activities that involve movement, crafts, sorting, and so forth. Although some of the activities provided in the "At a Glance" document for the project include using digital apps, the intent of this component is to have children engage in activities that build upon previous learning but are not related to technology.

◊ Family Focus: A list of online early literacy resources in English with Spanish translations is provided. The intent of these resources is to provide caregivers with parenting information related to fostering traditional literacy skills. Information sources include ¡Colorín Colorado!, National Association for the Education of Young Children (NAEYC), Raising Readers, and Reading Is Fundamental.

◊ Free Play: A list of interactive gaming and play apps are provided for children to explore either independently or with their parents. Children are encouraged to simply play with these apps and no specific guiding questions or activities are given. Apps include *Toca Hair, Toca House, Seed Cycle, Paint with Time,* and *Dress Chica,* to name a few.

Additional information about the Comienza en Casa program, including lists of activities, recommended apps, photographs, and samples of children's work is available at www.manomaine.org/comienzaencasa. This program has potential for fostering cultural competence if it is modified to include bilingual children's books representing diverse cultural groups as well as apps with cultural content. It is also important to include activities that allow children and their parents to explore their own and other cultures, and to provide opportunities to make intercultural connections.

Early Learning Collaborative—Pocoyo

In 2013 the U.S. Department of Education's Office of Innovation and Improvement provided grant funding to the Hispanic Information and Telecommunications Network (HITN) for the multifaceted Early Learning Collaborative (ELC) initiative, which combines digital media, outreach, and research to help prepare three- to five-year-old children for school readiness. One part of the ELC initiative is a program that uses digital tablets and specially designed "playsets" featuring the international children's program character Pocoyo to teach early literacy, math, and English language skills to

Spanish-speaking children in the United States. The program's goal is to use a combination of interactive educational apps that employ learning games, songs, and digital stories to close the learning gap between preschoolers in low-income and high-income households. Included on the program's website (http://earlylearningcollaborative.org/) is a seven-page toolkit to assist educators in integrating the Pocoyo apps and digital tablets into various parts of the preschool curriculum. The premise of the program, much like Comienza en Casa, is to provide learning opportunities that take children from tablet screen to printed reading materials to hands-on learning activities and back to the tablet for more interactive learning. The major differ-

Allison Tran on Virtual Puppets and Digital Play in Library Storytimes

Allison Tran, youth services librarian at the Mission Viejo Library in Southern California, uses digital apps to create storytime aides. In February 2012 she created a sock puppet storytime "rules" digital video entitled Sock Puppet Storytime Guidelines (http://youtu.be/ckHYFcb9NwA). Allison developed the video as an experimental way to deliver a potentially negative message—the rules of storytime. She notes, "I like to foster a positive atmosphere in my storytimes, to ensure that my attendees feel warm and welcome, and no matter how nicely I think I'm delivering the rules, I always feel a little worried that I might be unknowingly alienating someone in the audience."

Allison acknowledges that not everyone (other librarians, caregivers, and children) may like her video. However, she believes that having the rules delivered by a cute character softens the message and sets a more relaxed tone for the program. While she admits that she likes the idea of using a real puppet to deliver the rules, she understands that librarians have their personal style when presenting storytimes, and puppets just aren't for everyone. She is a firm believer that a storytime performance has to be authentic, and if a librarian can't buy into the use of something, then the audience also won't buy it. "So, puppets aren't my thing," Allison remarks, "but I do have voiceover experience, and I absolutely love creating characters. When I found the Sockpuppets app, I felt like, hey, this is something I could use creatively and comfortably! It fits my personal presentation style."

ence between the two programs is ELC's focus on classroom learning (child literacy) and Comienza en Casa's focus on home family learning (family literacy). At the time of this writing, the Pocoyo project was in the pilot test phase with Spanish-speaking preschoolers in multiple states including Alabama, California, Florida, Maine, and New York. The other part of the ELC initiative, still in the design phase, is Ready To Learn (RTL), which uses children's book character Miss Spider to teach digital literacy using transmedia storytelling. Information about the program's progress is available at http://projectlamp.org/. In addition to the Pocoyo and Miss Spider programs, ELC is funded to conduct research on how young children in-

She agrees with other children's librarians that learning through physical interactions with people and objects is vital to child development. She also does not think screens are a substitute for real experiences. She is an advocate for children learning and engaging with the world through non-digital means, but the families in her community are heavy users of digital tablets and smartphones. She would rather model healthy joint engagement with digital media than see parents handing the iPad to their toddlers in the stroller while they tap away on their smartphone. In essence, she is doing what all responsive children's librarians do: meeting the needs of her community.

Her Sock Puppet Storytime Guidelines video takes up 42 seconds of a 25-minute storytime that typically involves several books, music and movement, sign language, and international languages and cultures. The app is not replacing anything other than Allison reciting some rules. Showing the video is a way of modeling content creation for her storytime attendees. Rather than diminishing her connection with storytime attendees, it's a moment where she can share something she made, and share information with parents about how they can engage with their children and make up a sock puppet story too. For Allison, this is a more positive way to connect with the parents than asking them to silence their cell phones. She is connecting with them to tell them about a creative resource they might use with their child.

Allison notes that the app is only one tool in the librarian's toolbox. It is not a one-size-fits-all solution for librarians. "Some of us like to deliver storytime rules verbally," she comments, "some of us like to make a poster, and some of us like to make a handout. It is important for librarians to play to our own strengths as we work to address the needs of our diverse communities."

Figure 5.2: Allison Tran on Virtual Puppets and Digital Play in Library Storytimes

teract with digital media to discern the best strategies for reaching the potential of digital media to foster successful early literacy development.

Digital Storytime Models

A growing number of libraries across the country have started planning and hosting digital storytime programs. Within this burgeoning area, notable examples stand out as model ideas and programs to help other librarians on

---

Sample Cultural Literacy Storytimes Incorporating Digital Media

Storytime Plan 1

Grade Range: PreK–1 (The stories here cover a wide range of ages.) Librarians can substitute alternative stories to meet the ages of their particular program.
Opening Song/Routine: Use whatever is standard for your storytime program.
Topic: Chickens and Multilingualism

Book 1:
Beautiful Yetta: The Yiddish Chicken by Daniel Pinkwater. Illustrated by Jill Pinkwater. Feiwel & Friends/Macmillan, 2010. Yetta, a Yiddish-speaking chicken, escapes her crate on the way to the butcher shop and finds herself alone on the streets of Brooklyn. With the help of other multilingual birds, she finally finds her way, introducing to children the important concept of making cross-cultural connections in the world. The text includes English, Hebrew, and Spanish.

Song:
Explain that the parrots in Yetta's story spoke Spanish and that many people throughout Latin America and Spain also speak Spanish. Children in these countries learn songs and rhymes as they grow up just like the children here. A popular children's rhyme in Latin American is "Los Pollitos *Dicen*/Baby Chicks Sing."
Teach the children the song "Los Pollitos Dicen/Baby Chicks Sing." Project the lyrics using the digital tablet and LCD projector. Lyrics and music score are available at Mama Lisa's World: http://www.mamalisa.com/?t=es&p=262&c=41. Stylized song sheets, actions cards, and additional sheet music are available at Canciones Infantiles: http://canciones-infantiles.com.es/cancion-los-pollitos-dicen/. Also print out copies of the song lyrics for the parents.

---

their journey to getting digital in the library. Allison Tran, youth services librarian at the Mission Viejo Library in Southern California, used one of the many sock puppet apps available to create a YouTube video (http://youtu.be/ckHYFcb9NwA) explaining library storytime rules to children and their caregivers. This ingenious idea is sure to hold the attention of program attendees and models a constructive way to use an app in a children's

Text continues on page 108

Book 2:
Señor Pancho Had a Rancho by René Colato Laínez. Illustrated by Elwood Smith. Holiday House, 2013. Old MacDonald and Señor Pancho have barnyards next to each other filled with animals. Unfortunately, the animals can't communicate at first because some speak Spanish and the others English. Eventually, they teach each other the different languages and live in harmony—singing harmony that is! Imbued with humor, the catchy narrative and energetic illustrations are perfect for read-aloud. Children will also notice that the chicks say pío, pío, pío as in the song they just learned.

Digital Learning:
App 1:
Felt Board. Software Smoothie. Resembling a real felt board and felt pieces, this interactive app has a multitude of uses for the children's library. For this particular storytime, project the app using the LCD projector. After modeling how to use it, have children come up and help you move pieces around on the app to retell the story of *Señor Pancho Had a Rancho*. Alternatively, engage in your own storytelling of one of the many chicken stories available and have children assist you with the felt board by placing pieces on the screen. Now have the children tell their own favorite chicken stories or recreate the "Los Pollitos" song using the felt board app on individual tablets.

App 2:
Sock Puppets. Smith Micro Software. Instead of using felt board, librarians can use the interactive Sock Puppet app to tell their favorite chicken story (modeling how to use the app) and then have the children use the app on individual tablets to retell their own chicken stories or songs.

Book 3 (Alternate Story):
The Problem with Chickens by Bruce McMillan. Illustrated by Gunnella. Set in Iceland, this light-hearted story follows a group of women who purchase some chickens to lay eggs for baking. Unfortunately, the more

Figure 5.3 continues on page 106

time the women and chickens spend together the more they act like each other. Librarians can substitute this story for *Señor Pancho* and lead the storytime in a different direction, discussing chicken tales and songs with characters from around the world

Take Home Digital Media Extension:
App 3:
Los Pollitos. Cantos. Perfect for bilingual Spanish-English storytimes, this musical app teaches young children the popular Latin American song "Los Pollitos *Dicen*/Baby Chicks Sing." Functionality includes several different options of singers in English and Spanish. Multiple hot spots encourage children to make each chick sing "pío, pío, pío" as well as facilitate interactions between the mother hen and her babies. Children and parents can play this app together, with the parent prompting the child to sing along. The parents can also ask what sound the baby chick makes. And the children can respond and make the baby chick sing. Children can demonstrate how the mother feeds her young. The sound can be turned off and children can tell a story based on the images on the screen and their interactions with the characters. For instance, "the baby chickens are hungry and want a bedtime story. Mama hen gets them food and tells them their favorite story. Once upon a time . . . ." In this scenario, children and caregivers are combining multiple elements from the library's storytime and extending learning.

Storytime Plan 2

Grade Range: 1–3
Opening Song/Routine: Use whatever is standard for your storytime program.
Topic: Introduce the topic of losing teeth. Ask who has lost a tooth or known someone who has lost a tooth. What happens when you lose a tooth? Where do you put it? Who comes and gets your tooth? Fairy? Explain that in some places in the world children don't put their tooth under a pillow and a fairy doesn't come and get it. Also explain that sometimes, a loose tooth has a mind of its own.

Book 1:
The Tooth Fairy Meets El Ratón Perez by René Colato Laínez. Illustrated by Tom Lintern. Tricycle Press, 2010. When Miguelito, a young Mexican American boy, loses his tooth, a fight ensues between El Ratón Perez and the Tooth Fairy over who will get it. In some Latin American countries a small rat takes children's teeth instead of a tooth fairy. Since Miguelito is bicultural, both tooth stealers think they have dibs.

Book app/e-book:
The Tooth That's on the Loose! by Chris Robertson. SachManya LLC. Using the KiteReaders app platform, this engaging, funny e-book follows wily tooth outlaw T.B. Wiggly who is on the run and must be captured. Various hotspots encourage children to interact with the illustrations. Librarians can display the book on a screen by connecting the digital tablet to an LCD projector. Children can come up and assist with various hotspots or the librarian can run the app solo.

Book 2:
Throw Your Tooth on the Roof: Tooth Traditions from Around the World by Selby Beeler. Illustrated by G. Brian Karas. Houghton Mifflin Harcourt, 1998. Explores what children around the world do when they lose a tooth.

Digital Learning Activity:
Educational App:
Barefoot World Atlas. Touch Press. With this interactive educational app, children can explore various cultures of the world learning geographical and cultural facts as well as exploring languages, art, and more. Divide children into groups (if you have a large group of children) or have children work with their parents. Have each group or parent/child team use the *Barefoot World Atlas* app to explore the country with the most interesting tooth tradition that was mentioned in *Throw Your Tooth on the Roof*. Provide a list of things to examine about the culture and have the children compare/contrast how they are the same and "same, but different" from children in the country explored. This will require that each group or parent/child team have their own tablet. If this is not available, use the world atlas as a group to explore some of the countries mentioned in Book 2.

Digital Media Extension:
This is an alternative activity that you can do if you only have a few digital tablets. Children can watch segments from this webstream while waiting their turn to use a tablet.
I Lost My Tooth in Africa Reading Rainbow webstream (http://vimeo. com/6493836). Librarians can go old-school with this vintage Reading Rainbow episode that introduces the picture book *I Lost My Tooth In Africa* by Penda Diakite. Illustrated by Baba Wague Diakite. Scholastic, 2006. This book follows a young American girl as she visits her extended family in Bamako, Mali. During the vacation, she loses her tooth, puts it under a gourd, and awaits the arrival of the African Tooth Fairy.

Figure 5.3: Sample Cultural Literacy Storytimes Incorporating Digital Media

library program. Families attending one of Allison's programs could later use a sock puppet app to record a retelling of books shared in storytime or to create their own story relating to the storytime theme.

Two youth services librarians in Colorado, Kate Lucey and Melissa Della Penna, developed digital storytime programs that incorporate the six early literacy skills described in the 2000 Every Child Ready to Read (ECRR) program along with the five supporting practices outlined in ECRR2, the second edition of ECRR, published in 2013. Their programs include traditional oral storytelling, songs, and hands-on tablet-based activities focused on counting, sequencing, and learning colors. In their online article "Once Upon an App: The Process of Creating Digital Storytimes for Preschoolers" published in *Colorado Libraries* (Lucey and Della Penna, 2012), the savvy librarians provide a model for developing digital storytimes, a survey instrument for gauging program success, and information on selecting the best apps.

Held in the children's department at the Southington (CT) Library and Museum, eTots: A Public Library iPad Program for Preschoolers is a digital storytime that includes singing songs, reading stories, exploring iPad storybook apps, and playing iPad educational game apps. The library supplies the iPads as well as instructions for caregivers on how to use the iPads and apps. An example of the program's flyer can be found at:

> http://southingtonkidsplace.files.wordpress.com/2012/06/etots-sign-2013.jpg.

Children's librarian Angela Reynolds from the Annapolis Valley (CA) Regional Library is a digital storytime diva, hosting multiple sessions of the digital storytime Tablet Tales in five branches throughout the system. The program includes apps, books, and hands-on literacy crafts, but particularly focuses on allowing families to play with and explore iPads to improve their digital literacy skills. Below is the program's marketing description from the library's website:

> Join us in exploring an app, a book, and a literacy craft that you can take home! At each session we will explore a new app. There will be time for each family to explore our iPads, hone their tablet skills, ask questions, and discover new learning apps at the end of each session. For families with children ages 3-6. Registration is limited, so please sign up if you are interested!

Additional information about Tablet Tales is also available in Angela's ALSC Blog Post "Getting Ready for Tablet Time" (Reynolds, 2014).

For basic information and considerations for starting up a digital storytime, librarians should consult Carissa Christner's *On Starting to Use Apps in Storytime*. Christner, a librarian at the Madison (WI) Public Library, gives basic, common sense suggestions for how to present an app to children during storytime. These include reviewing the app ahead of time, emphasizing the connection to early literacy skills, saying the name of the app during the program, and deciding delivery style. This is available at http://littleelit.com/2014/02/21/on-starting-to-use-apps-in-storytime-by-carissa-christner/.

One of the best resources for conceptualizing digital storytimes in libraries is Jennifer Gal's "Digital Storytime: Preschool Programming with the iPad" (http://www.slideshare.net/Jennifer.Gal/digital-story-time-sols-feb-14-2013-jennifer-gal). Gal, a librarian at the Hamilton (Ontario) Public Library, describes in this highly informative presentation the equipment needed for digital storytimes and how to select the best apps. She also provides an overview of what occurs in a digital storytime and why digital apps are good to use with children.

The most comprehensive resource for finding dynamic examples digital storytime programs and models in the library is the Programming with Apps section of the Little eLit website (http://littleelit.com/programming-with-apps/). Several examples of storytime lesson plans and models used in libraries across the nation are profiled. Librarians are encouraged to choose the model or program plan that works best for their library.

Putting It All Together

Using a program format adapted from the model by Angela Reynolds, youth services manager at the Annapolis Valley Regional Library, and posted on Little eLit, I have created a few storytime lesson plans that combine digital media with global children's books to promote cultural competence. Librarians can use these plans as springboards for their own creative programming. I have also created a few examples of book and digital media pairings to demonstrate in a less formal manner how the two formats can be put together for culturally competent digital storytimes. See Figure 5.3 for sample storytime lesson plans and Figure 5.4 for media pairings. Additional

Text continues on page 112

Sample Digital Media and Book Pairings to Promote Cultural Competence

Sample 1:

Garza, Xavier. *Maximilian and the Mystery of the Guardian Angel: A Bilingual Lucha Libre Thriller.* El Paso, TX: Cinco Puntos Press, 2011. 207 pp. Audience: Grades 3–6. ISBN: 978-1-933693-98-9. Awards: Belpré Honor Book, 2012; ALA Notable Children's Book, 2012. Cultures Depicted: Mexican, Mexican American.

Eleven-year-old Max is a huge fan of lucha libre wrestling; he particularly likes the masked luchador called the Guardian Angel. While at one of the Guardian Angel's wrestling matches with his Uncle Lalo, Max discovers that his uncle and the Guardian Angel look very much alike. Soon the boy discovers that the Guardian Angel is his mother's long-lost brother, thought to be dead. The Guardian Angel decides that he'd like for someone to carry on the luchador tradition in the family—will it be Lalo or Max? The perfect title for reluctant readers, Max's adventure provides an opportunity for young people to learn about Mexican wrestling and make intercultural connections with wrestlers and heroes from other cultures. The book also contains references to Latino folklore, which could be explored with folklore from around the world.

Other Suggested Titles:

◊ *Lucha Libre: The Man in the Silver Mask* by Xavier Garza (Grades 1–3)

◊ *My Father, the Angel of Death* by Ray Villareal (Grades 5–up)

◊ *Sumo* by Thien Pham (Grades 5–up)

◊ *Maximilian and the Bingo Rematch: A Lucha Libre Sequel* by Xavier Garza (Grades 3–6)

◊ *Niño Wrestles the World* by Yuyi Morales (Grades PreK–2)

Digital Media Tie-In:

◊ *Lucha Libre USA: Make Your Own Masked Warrior* app by Night & Day Studios, Inc.

◊ *Lucha Libre Mask* app by Purple Penguin.com

◊ *Rock vs. Paper vs. Scissors Rumble—A Challenging Puzzle Game* app by Continuous Integration

Programming Ideas:

◊ Lucha Libre Toilet Paper Roll Craft (online pattern)—http://www.dltk-kids. com/world/mexico/mluchalibre.htm

◊ How to make a lucha libre mask out of a tee shirt (online blog post and pattern)—http://www.1up.com/do/blogEntry?bId=8835067

◊ Visit from local wrestling team

◊ WWF vs. Lucha Libre vs. Sumo wrestling

Topics: Wrestling, Latinos, Mexican Americans, Family Life, Heroes, Lucha Libre, Spanish-Language Materials.

Sample 2:

Kostecki-Shaw, Jenny Sue. *Same, Same But Different*. New York: Henry Holt, 2011. 36 pp. Audience: Grades K–up. ISBN: 978-0-8050-8946-2. Awards: Ezra Jack Keats New Illustrator Award, 2012; Ezra Jack Keats New Author Honor Award, 2012. Cultures Depicted: American, Indian.

Elliot and Kailash are pen pals from two very different worlds. Through letters and detailed, cheerful illustrations children follow these two boys as they learn how the lives of an American boy and an Indian boy are different but the same. Both go to school, have families, play games, etc. The universality of daily life is shared, demonstrating that we are all the same, same but different. The book has cross-appeal for multiple age groups, allowing children to explore a variety of topics relating to the lives of children in other countries. Programs using the book could cover social activism, world storytelling, geography explorations, global pen pals, and more.

Other Suggested Titles:

◊ *This Child, Every Child: A Book About the World's Children* (CitizenKid) by David J. Smith and Shelagh Armstrong (Grades 2–6)

◊ *I Have the Right to Be a Child* by Alain Serres, Aurelia Fronty, and Helen Mixter (Grades K–3)

◊ *The Sandwich Swap* by Queen Rania of Jordan Al Abdullah, Kelly DiPucchio, and Tricia Tusa (Grades K–2)

◊ *Let's Talk About Race* by Julius Lester and Karen Barbour (Grades 3–6)

◊ *We All Sing with the Same Voice* by J. Philip Miller, Sheppard M. Greene, and Paul Meisel (Grades PreK–1)

◊ *Whoever You Are* by Mem Fox and Leslie Staub (Grades PreK–1)

Figure 5.4 continues on page 112

- *Off to Class: Incredible and Unusual Schools Around the World* by Susan Hughes (Grades 2–5)

- *My Librarian Is a Camel: How Books Are Brought to Children Around the World* by Margriet Ruurs (Grades 2–6)

Digital Media Tie-In:

- *Being Global* app by SachManya LLC and Little Pickle Press

- *One Globe Kids: Children's Stories from Around the World* app by Round By Design

- *Up and Down* app by Mr. Garamond

- *Touchable Earth* app by Touchable Earth

Programming Ideas:

- Discuss the United Nations Declaration of the Rights of the Child and brainstorm how children can take a stand to help other children in the

Text continued from page 109

suggestions of books to pair with specific digital media for cultural programming can be found in Chapter 7.

Conclusion

This chapter has provided examples of cultural literacy programs as well as glimpses into what effective, high-quality digital storytimes look like. Some librarians may find it easier to integrate digital media into existing cultural literacy programs such as Día rather than creating separate digital storytimes. Other librarians may want to establish separate digital storytimes that include multicultural digital media to cultivate cultural competence. Use whatever seems natural and works for you.

References

American Library Association. (2014). "ALA Family Literacy Focus." Accessed February 12, 2014, at http://www.ala.org/advocacy/literacy/earlyliteracy/famlitfocus.

American Library Association Muslim Journeys. (2013). "Muslim Journeys Bookshelf." Accessed February 17, 2014, at http://www.

world. Child-friendly version of the declaration available at http://www.
unicef.org/rightsite/484_540.htm

◊ ePals (http://www.epals.com/#!/global-community/)—Librarians can
connect children with other children their own age for pen pal projects,
book discussions of any of the afore-mentioned titles, and more.

◊ Sole Hope Project (http://www.solehope.org/)—Social activism project.
Host a shoe cutting party where children cut out shoe patterns from
fabric to mail to Sole Hope to help make shoes for children who don't
have them.

◊ Peace Corp for Kids (http://www.peacecorps.gov/kids/)—Social activism
game teaching about children around the world.

◊ Free Rice (http://freerice.com/)—Non-profit website supporting the
United Nations World Food Programme. The global awareness game
donates free food to starving families based on online participation.

Figure 5.4: Sample Digital Media and Book Pairings to Promote Cultural Competence

programminglibrarian.org/muslimjourneys/about/mj-about-
bookshelf.html.

Larson, Jeanette. *El día de los niños/El día de los libros: Building a Culture
of Literacy in Your Community through Día.* Chicago: American
Library Association, 2011.

Lepman, Jella. *A Bridge of Children's Books: The Inspiring Autobiography
of a Remarkable Woman.* Dublin: The O'Brien Press, 2002.
(Originally published in German in 1964 by Fischer as *Die
Kinderbuchbrücke.*)

Lucey, Kate, and Melissa Della Penna. (2012). "Once Upon an App: The
Process of Creating Digital Storytimes for Preschoolers." *Colorado
Libraries* 36, no. 3. Accessed February 19, 2014, at http://www.
coloradolibrariesjournal.org/articles/once-upon-app-process-
creating-digital-storytimes-preschoolers.

Mora, Pat. "Foreword." In *El día de los niños/El día de los libros: Building
a Culture of Literacy in Your Community Through Día* (pp. 7-9).
Chicago: American Library Association, 2011.

Reynolds, Angela. (February 20, 2014). "Getting Ready for Tablet Time."
ALSC Blog. Accessed February 20, 2014, at http://www.alsc.ala.org/
blog/2014/02/getting-ready-for-tablet-time/.

Chapter 6

Criteria for Selecting and Evaluating Culturally Responsive Media

With contribution from Sarah Park Dahlen

> In many parts of the world children were holding books in their hands and meeting over a bridge of children's books. And all this was only a start. The possibilities were without limit. (Lepman, 2002/1964, p. 154)

In 1964 global literacy pioneer Jella Lepman speculated about the possibilities that global children's literature held for connecting children from diverse cultures. She dreamed of a world where children from all countries and cultures were united and culturally competent as a result of literary interactions. Books were just the beginning. If she were alive today, Lepman would likely embrace the idea of children using digital media (particularly in the form of interactive digital picture books) to connect with each other and build bridges of understanding. Indeed, renowned educational psychology scholar Howard Gardner and colleague Katie Davis suggest that well-chosen digital media in the form of apps can serve as these very bridges of understanding when used in moderation and with a directed purpose. Gardner and Davis note, "As portals to the world, apps can broaden young people's awareness of and access to experiences and identities beyond their immediate environment" (2013, p. 91).

When carefully selected and used in moderation, high-quality digital media representing cultural diversity have the potential to foster cultural competence in children, connecting them to the experiences of diverse children around the globe. Digital media are increasingly social, and this allows children to interact with people who are not located geographically close to them. However, it is important to remember that not all of these materials are created equally. Numerous other resources describe how to evaluate various print materials for children, so we will not cover that here. Rather, we will focus on how to select and evaluate digital media in general and then specifically how to select culturally affirming print and digital media for culturally competent programming.

General Criteria for Evaluating Digital Media

One of the most helpful sets of criteria for evaluating digital media such as websites, digital picture books, and apps in general comes from the Association for Library Service to Children (ALSC). ALSC's Great Websites for Kids Selection Criteria give basic guidelines for ensuring that the content of digital media is developmentally appropriate, accurate, and easy to navigate. Established in 1997 by the ALSC Children and Technology Committee and updated in 2013 by the ALSC Great Websites Committee, the criteria include the following:

- *Authorship/Sponsorship.* Identifying who created a particular type of digital media and their authority in the subject matter.
- *Purpose.* Discerning why a particular digital media was created and its goal.
- *Design and Stability.* Evaluating how children can access and use the content and ensuring that it is easy to navigate, compliant with the Americans with Disabilities Act, updated regularly, free of excess clutter, and loads easily.
- *Content.* Analyzing the information to ensure accuracy, developmental appropriateness, correct grammar and spelling, bias-free images and text, advertisement-free material, and privacy protection.

The full guidelines, including examples of high-quality websites for children, are available at http://gws.ala.org/about/selection-criteria.

A particular concern when evaluating children's digital media is advertising. In-app advertising can be problematic, particularly if credit card or purchasing information is loaded and unlocked in the tablet's cloud. With a few clicks, children may end up purchasing toys, music, other apps, and more! An example of this can be seen in the children's book app *A Song for Miles* created by Tiffany Russell and Diverse Mobile, LLC. On the surface, the concept of the app is laudable as it follows a young African American boy as he learns more about various black musicians. However, within the app are hyperlinks that transport readers to iTunes to purchase music created by the various profiled artists. Unless this feature is disabled, a child left unattended may purchase an extensive discography of songs.

When considering children's digital media such as streaming video or film, librarians can consult the Charter for Children's Television. Initially presented by Anna Home at the First World Summit on Children and Television in March 1995 and later amended at the Second World Summit, the Charter for Children's Television outlines what types of digital content are appropriate for children. This information is particularly applicable to streaming video/film but can be applied to almost all children's digital media. According to the charter:

◊ Children should have programs of high quality which are made specifically for them, and which do not exploit them. These programs, in addition to entertaining, should allow children to develop physically, mentally, and socially to their fullest potential.

◊ Children should hear, see and express themselves, their culture, their language, and their life experiences, through . . . programs which affirm their sense of self, community and place.

◊ Children's programs should promote an awareness and appreciation of other cultures in parallel with the child's own cultural background.

◊ Children's programs should be wide-ranging in genre and content, but should not include gratuitous scenes of violence and sex. (Home, 1995, par. 3)

Specific Criteria for Evaluating Apps

Developmentally appropriate, interactive, and engaging apps are the key to successful library programming with apps. When considering an app to use in a library program, it is important to explore and evaluate the app before integrating it into a story program. Just as a children's librarian would not read a book during storytime without first reading it aloud to himself or herself, the same librarian would not want to feature an app in a storytime without first learning about its functionality, evaluating its ease of use, and analyzing its depiction of genders and cultural groups.

Simon and Nemeth (2012) provide a helpful list of things to avoid when selecting an app to use with young children. These include avoiding apps that: are not interactive, serve as boring flashcards or coloring sheets, bombard children with in-app advertising and promotions, provide one-dimensional activities with no challenge, serve as opportunities to market a product, and have functionality that is too complicated for children to understand. Falloon (2013) also describes features that apps should include to be most useful in educational settings. Apps should be:

- communicating learning objectives in ways young students can access and understand;
- providing smooth and distraction-free pathways towards achieving goals;
- including accessible and understandable instructions and teaching elements;
- incorporating formative, corrective feedback;
- combining an appropriate blend of game, practice and learning components;
- providing interaction parameters matched to the learning characteristics of the target student group (i.e., developmentally appropriate). (Falloon, 2013, p. 519)

Apps including these features have the *potential* for productive learning experiences. Potential is stressed here because how the apps are used truly determines whether they help students achieve learning goals. If apps are to be used independently by children, rather than in a librarian-led activity such as storytime, then the app content and features should be open-ended rather than with a specific answer like rote memorization or drill activities (Kucirkova et al., 2014). Apps that are open-ended tend to facilitate creativity and peer collaboration and "foster several desirable outcomes, including higher educational engagement and exploratory talk, which are associated with joint problem solving skills and academic success" (Kucirkova et al., 2014, p. 183). This is particularly important to keep in mind when selecting the "App of the Day" for standalone kiosks on shelf end caps such as those at the Darien (CT) Public Library.

Rather than rushing to adopt an app for use in a library program, it is important to consider what it adds to the learning experience. Simon and

Nemeth (2012) suggest, "if you wouldn't offer a similar corresponding traditional activity (like worksheets or flash cards), that app is inappropriate" (p. 84). Recommended types of apps for use with children individually in the library or during storytime include the following:

- interactive storybook/picture book apps, particularly those that are bilingual, that allow children to either read the story themselves or have the story read to them. These apps should also have functionality that sounds out words for children and includes purposeful interactions that do not detract from the narrative

- musical apps such as *Drum Circle Kids* that turn an iPad or other tablet into a drum, maraca, piano, or other musical instrument apps such as *Sock Puppets* that record children's voices and allow them to make their own stories and reader's theatre

- creative apps allowing children to paint, draw, record sounds, create comic strips, etc.

- song apps that allow librarians to play songs that complement the program and may include multiple languages

Good apps will provide opportunities for children to explore stories and activities in a variety of languages. The language a child speaks, reads, and comprehends comprises a part of his or her culture. Apps meant to teach children new languages should rely on the same vetted methodologies used in teaching children literacy in their primary language. Apps that have the potential for helping children make cross-cultural connections might have functionality that includes bilingual text. When thinking about selecting bilingual apps for children, Nemeth (2012) offers a comprehensive list of questions to consider:

1 What languages are available?
   - Are additional languages free?
   - Provided via in-app purchase?
   - Available by downloading or purchasing different versions?

2 What is the complexity of the language used in the app?
   - One word at a time?
   - Simple vocabulary that is traditional for preschool but adds little to the child's ability to communicate or process knowledge (like names of animals, shapes, or colors)
   - Sentences?

- Stories/songs?
- Complex activities that require thought and response?

3 In what language was the app written?

- Was the app written in English, then translated?
- Was the app developed in another language, then translated to English?
- Does the developer offer any documentation to support the accuracy of the translation?
- Is the whole app available in the two languages?
- Are the instructions in English, and some of the activity is provided in another language?

4 Is there any way for the app to grow with the child?

- Are there multiple levels?
- Is there a way to track what the child has learned or accomplished?

5 Does the app meet with Developmentally Appropriate Practice?

- Does the app take a flashcard approach?
- Does the app engage the child in activity such as singing or solving puzzles or problems?
- Are there opportunities for children to choose, plan, or create?

6 Are the images and activities culturally appropriate and free of stereotypes?

7 Is there a way to record the child's productive language in the context of the app? (Nemeth, 2012, par. 5)

Bircher (2012) provides a concise list of qualities that successful picture-book apps should embody. These recommended features can easily guide a librarian's evaluation when deciding which picture-book apps to use in children's programming. Her suggestions include the following:

- *Interactive but not too interactive.* If an app has too much interactivity, readers will become distracted from the narratives by the various hotspots and embedded games.

- *Meaningful counterpoints between all features of the app.* "Every aspect of an app—text, images, narration, music and sound effects, and interactive enhancements—should be accessible and enjoyable, not distracting. The features should also be interdependent, creating an experience greater than the sum of an app's parts." (Bircher, 2012, par. 5)

◊ *Dramatic page turns.* Even though digital books don't have physical pages, a successful picture book app will give the same sense of dramatic page turns as a print picture book.

◊ *Puts users in charge.* An app should have customizable options that fit the needs of diverse users and allow them to manipulate the content to create the best environment for individualized literacy explorations.

◊ *Easy to navigate.* Successful apps are intuitive by design, easy to navigate, and are not condescending when giving instructions.

◊ *Offers surprising and joyful experiences.* "Effective apps balance interactive moments that propel the story forward with others that are just pure fun—but feel natural to the story's setting and characters." (Bircher, 2012, par. 15)

◊ *Withstands repeated use.* Good picture-book apps have multiple storylines and features that can be manipulated during repeated use to create different stories and experiences.

◊ *Extends the existing print book.* Picture-book apps should not replace a printed book. Rather, they should be used to extend the storyline and provide additional literacy experiences.

Another important evaluative tool for examining apps and other digital media for children is accessibility. All media should strive to meet universal access standards so that users of all abilities can fully enjoy their functionality. According to the World Wide Web Consortium (W3C) Web Content Accessibility Guidelines (WCAG) 2.0 (http://www.w3.org/TR/WCAG20/), websites, apps, and other digital media meet universal access standards when they are perceivable, operable, understandable, and robust. These characteristics are further explained below.

◊ *Perceivable.* A perceivable website or app is one that can be read through alternative means such as a screen reader. The xhtml and css coding of the website must be written in such a way that a screen reader can locate headers, body, alternative captions for images, and so on. Without the proper labels embedded within xhtml, a screen reader would read all the text without explaining that something was a header or a footer. The human reader may then be confused when hearing a phrase or incomplete sentence, and would also not know when he or she should move on to the next page. For people with low vision contrast, a perceivable website is one that is designed

Developing High-Quality Apps for Children

D evelopers of recommended, high-quality children's apps put considerable effort into creating developmentally appropriate activities; kid-friendly navigational commands; visually appealing graphics, fonts, and illustrations; and age-appropriate instructions, social messages, and narratives. Culturally sensitive app developers will also consider how particular cultures are being depicted throughout the app and ensure that the multilingual language options are grammatically correct and include accurate pronunciations. For dedicated developers, there are numerous resources available to assist in creating a good children's app. Many of these resources have information useful to librarians and educators interested in learning more about what makes a high-quality app for children.

According to its website (http://www.bookappalliance.com/), the Book App Alliance (BAA) aspires to be the "leading community of innovative book app authors working together to share resources that will help bring awareness of high-quality book apps to the world." A particular emphasis of the consortium of children's book and app creators is to help parents and educators understand the role that apps can play in a child's educational journey. BAA also provides resources for children's authors interested in developing apps, particularly those authors interested in making their print book digital.

Another detailed resource for developers of children's apps is Sesame Street's *Best Practices: Designing Touch Tablet Experiences for Preschoolers,* which provides many helpful tips and researcher suggestions on how to design developmentally appropriate and engaging digital media for young children. While aimed at app developers, the guidelines can also serve as a checklist for librarians and other educators interested in selecting apps for digital storytimes. An abbreviated report is available at the following URL with an additional link to the full report: http://www.sesameworkshop.org/our-blog/2012/12/17/sesames-best-practices-guide-for-childrens-app-development/.

An equally useful resource for librarians, educators, and other adults interested in what it takes to create high-quality digital media for children are the "Quality Conversations Articles" published by the Fred Rogers Center for Early Learning and Children's Media. These articles examine the educational uses of apps and e-books with young children and pose important questions about media usage. The articles in the series include *Are All E-Books Created Equal?, How Can Apps Cultivate Creativity in Young Children?, Can Apps Encourage Parents and Kids to Use Media Together?,* and *What Do Quality Children's Apps Look Like?* (http://www.

fredrogerscenter.org/blog/category/quality-conversations)

Children's book authors looking to extend their reach to connect with digital natives might consider creating an e-book or book app version of their printed book. However, many authors don't have the skills to do this and need guidance. Numerous companies exist to help authors create digital book media. One example is Kids App Creator (http://kidsappcreator.com/), a Belgian company that works with book publishers or individual children's book creators to turn printed books into interactive book apps. Various global children's book publishers have used this company to expand the audience of their books by making them interactive apps. Equally important in creating children's apps is compliance with the Children's Online Privacy Protection Act (COPPA). Set forth by the Federal Trade Commission in the 1990s, the act was updated in 2013 to include apps developed for children. Essentially the act limits the type of personal information that developers can collect from children and requires that parents have control over what information is collected about their child while using the app. Some children's authors and app developers may become overwhelmed by what they can and can't do in relation to COPPA. In *Designing Apps for Children: Guide to COPPA and Mobile Apps,* a consulting company provides basic information on how COPPA influences children's app development) https://www.iubenda.com/blog/2013/09/24/guide-coppa-mobile-apps/).

For more information about developing digital apps for children, including interviews and market snapshots, check out the following resources.

"Once Upon a Time . . . An Overview of the Children's Book App Market" by Julie Brannon. *Digital Media Diet* (http://digitalmediadiet. com/?p=1080).

"A Brief History of StoryApps and Interactivity" by Sarah Towle (http:// www.youtube.com/watch?v=z_1Elo6-Qfs).

"What Makes a Good Picturebook App?" by Katie Bircher. *Horn Book* (http://www.hbook.com/2012/02/using-books/what-makes-a-good-picture-book-app).

"An Interview with App Designer Roxie" by ALSC Digital Content Taskforce. *ALSC Blog* (http://www.alsc.ala.org/blog/2013/03/an-interview-with-book-app-designer-roxie/).

"App Storytime: PBBC Chats with Michel Kripalani, the President of Oceanhouse Media Inc, About Creating Children's Book Apps" by Phoenix Baby Book Club (http://phoenixbabybookclub.blogspot. com/2013/02/app-storytime-pbbc-chats-with-michel.html).

Figure 6.1: Developing High-Quality Apps for Children

with high contrast colors for its text and images. This is especially important if a website or app is designed for interactivity that is based on different colors. For someone who is hearing impaired, a universal website or app is one in which the sound functionality can be experienced through an alternative means, such as a caption. The caption must be descriptive enough for someone to understand when it is dealing with a sound rather than writing out a statement.

- *Operable.* An operable website or app is one that is functional using different senses, such as vision or hearing. It must also allow for sufficient timing between actions. One important trait of an operable website or app is that the motions on the screen do not cause seizures among users who are sensitive to movement. Another very important trait of an operable website or app is navigation. Users should be able to understand how to move around easily on the app with little prompting.

- *Understandable.* Related to *navigation* under the *operable* category, a website or app must be designed so that the next steps are logical and intuitive. A website or app has been poorly designed if there are no indicators for a user's next steps. It then follows that whether or not an app is intuitive in its navigation, users should be given an "undo" option so as to retrace their steps and begin again. This may vary depending on the structure and goal of the app, but allowing users to fix their mistakes before progressing through a game, reading, or other activity may help them to practice trial and error before moving on. Of course, an app or website must at its core be readable and understandable in both its format and content. Writing for a screen and writing for the printed page are different, so app and website designers must consider when paragraphs are too lengthy, or when they are not taking the best advantage of the added functionality of digital media.

- *Robust.* An app, website, or other form of digital media must be robust and compatible with multiple platforms so as to be accessible to a wide array of users. To keep from becoming irrelevant, digital media must also be frequently updated to incorporate new research and user feedback.

Digital tablets such as the iPad have many universal design features built in such as voiceover, speak selection, speak auto-text, mono audio, zoom, font resize, contrast white on black, page brightness, assistive touch, and triple-click home shortcut. Built-in functionality may or may not be overridden by an app. If apps are designed with texts on jpg images, the iPad's built-in voiceover may not be able to read the text for someone who is vision-impaired. Similarly, the zoom-in/zoom-out functionality of the iPad can be lost if the text is static and part of a jpg image.

Selecting Culturally Affirming Print and Digital Media

According to Ito et al., "Digital media take the form they do because they are created by existing social and cultural contexts, contexts that are diverse and stratified" (2008, p. ix). As such, digital media are embedded with the cultural mores and beliefs of the app developers and content creators (authors, artists, designers, and so on). Whenever children interact with a specific app, e-book, digital picture book, or website, they encounter various overt and covert social and cultural scripts. These scripts influence how children perceive their culture, their classmates' cultures, and other global cultures. Stereotypes in digital media can create misunderstandings about particular cultures. Sadly, the unfortunate propensity to caricature non-white cultures in cartoons lends itself too easily to stereotyping in digital media.

Digital media are easier to produce and promote than print media because of the ease in developing and sharing apps. As editors of the John D. and Catherine T. MacArthur Foundation Series on Digital Media and Learning write, "Digital media have escaped the boundaries of professional and formal practice" (Ito et al., 2008, vii), implying that non-professionals are now participating in the creation, distribution, and use of digital media. Self-published works have been criticized for a lack of formal editing and refining, but digital media creation may undergo no such process at all. Because issues of racism, stereotyping, whitewashing, and other social concerns are still hot topics in children's and young adult literature, we must be similarly cautious about the presence of these issues in digital media. Conversations regarding these "hot button" issues have been ongoing since before Nancy Larrick's (1965) article, "The All-White World of Children's Books," and we have no reason to believe that the digital media industry is any more socially conscious than the children's book industry. We would like to believe otherwise, but a glance through the iTunes store reveals that most apps are created with a monocultural child in mind—the white, middle-class child. Essentially the "All-White World of Children's Books" with the aid of digital enhancements has now morphed into the "All-White

World of Children's Apps." While some culturally sensitive apps and other digital media are available to help them explore global cultures, children are predominantly exposed to apps with an embedded, socially constructed script perpetuating the notion of a singular culturally generic experience. As in the children's literature world, this generic experience generally represents white, middle-class culture. An app about a seemingly innocuous bunny going to school is by societal default an app about a white, middle-class child going to school. On the surface, this is may not seem bad; but if all the print and digital media that a child encounters depicts only white culture, then he or she learns that white, middle-class culture is superior to all other cultures. As such, in order to prepare our children to succeed in a culturally pluralistic, global society, it is extremely important to provide opportunities for cross-cultural connections through print and digital media representing diverse cultural experiences.

Specific Criteria for Examining Cultural Depictions in Children's Media

While numerous resources and checklists have been provided over the years to assist librarians and educators as they choose culturally diverse literature for children, the source most often referred to and the source that often forms the foundation for other evaluative tools is the Council on Interracial Books for Children's (CIBC's) classic *Ten Quick Ways to Analyze Children's Books for Sexism and Racism*. Although originally written for application to print materials, these guidelines are equally applicable to digital media with slight modifications. The ten ways cited by the CIBC (1980) are adapted below:

- *Check the Illustrations/Images.* Examine the illustrations in print books and images in digital media to identify any stereotypes or tokenism relating to particular cultural groups. Do culturally diverse characters play an actual role, or are they only a multicultural face in the background?

- *Check the Storyline or Narrative Material.* Examine the text of printed books or digital media to discern the standards for success, how problems are solved, and the role of females. What standards for success are overtly or covertly described? Who defines these standards? How are problems resolved? Does a "white savior" have to fix the problems of people from other cultures? Also examine the storyline or narrative to determine how genders are portrayed. Are males the strong figures while females are portrayed as weak? Are diverse genders represented in multiple roles and activities?

- *Look at Character Lifestyles.* Analyze the print or digital product to determine what cultural assumptions are projected about characters who don't fit the unstated norm (white, heterosexual, fully abled, Christian). Determine how different social classes are depicted and identify any bias against lower socioeconomic individuals.

- *Weigh the Relationships Between People.* Examine the text of printed books or digital media to discern if any particular cultural group has power over another, making all the decisions and exhibiting leadership roles. Are particular cultural groups depicted as not succeeding because of their class, ability, sexual orientation, religion, race, immigration status, or ethnicity?

- *Note the Heroes.* Examine the storyline, narrative, illustrations, and graphics to determine who the heroes are and who defines these heroes. Is a minority character a hero because he or she does something good for a majority character?

- *Consider the Effect on a Child's Self-Image.* Evaluate the digital or print product to determine what social messages about particular cultures are being relayed and discern if these messages are negative or positive. Think about how a child from the culture being presented would feel after engaging with the material. Would they be embarrassed or proud? Does the material reinforce cultural misconceptions?

- *Consider the Creator's Background.* How is the author, illustrator, designer, developer, or other contributor qualified to create media about a particular cultural group? Does the creator have experience with the culture represented? Is the creator representative of the culture depicted?

- *Determine the Creator's Perspective.* Is the author, illustrator, designer, developer, or other contributor creating the product using a specific lens: feminist, Eurocentric, classicist, and so forth. How does the creator's perspective influence the depiction of cultural diversity in the digital or print product?

- *Watch for Loaded Words.* Identify any loaded words used to describe minority characters such as *strange, lazy, backwards, retarded, savage, crafty, queer,* etc. Look for language that perpetuates sexism or gender stereotypes such as describing a girl as a tomboy or butch if she participates in male-stereotyped activities. Examine narratives for gender-neutral terms such as *chairperson* instead of *chairman*.

◊ *Look at the Copyright Date.* Older printed children's materials may be more likely to include bias than newer books. As most digital media are relatively recent, the copyright date guideline is not so relevant.

Application of the Council on Interracial Books for Children's *Ten Quick Ways* to a digital app can be seen in Figure 6.2. Librarians, educators, and caregivers using the CIBC guidelines may not be able to apply all ten of these factors to a particular product. Rather, they may choose the ones most applicable to gain an overall understanding of how an app portrays various cultures.

For example, the interactive app *Bunny Fun: Head, Shoulders, Knees, and Toes* created by Rosemary Wells and developed by Auryn Inc. doesn't have a storyline, portray character relationships, or depict any heroes. However, adults can evaluate the digital app's illustrations, consider the effect on a child's self-image, and determine the creators' background and perspective. The premise of the interactive educational app is to take children's author-illustrator Rosemary Well's beloved bunny characters and use them to teach children the song "Head, Shoulders, Knees, and Toes" in English, French, Spanish, and Japanese. Children can touch the various body parts of four different bunnies and hear the corresponding word for *head, shoulders, knees,* and *toes* in the four different languages. At the same time, children can select an option to hear the song sung in each of the languages and record themselves singing the song or saying the words in English, French, Spanish, or Japanese. The actions seem developmentally appropriate and purposeful for the intended audience of young children. The colors of the graphics and illustrations are vibrant and the navigation is easy to understand.

However, for some inexplicable reason Wells chooses to dress the English-speaking bunny in a cowboy outfit and place him in the desert. The French-speaking bunny is dressed in a sailor outfit in the colors of the French flag and is standing on a floating boat in front of the Eiffel Tower while the Spanish-speaking bunny is wearing a mariachi outfit and standing in an adobe house with a piñata hanging from the rafters. Finally, the Japanese-speaking bunny is dressed in a kimono and standing in front of what appears to be a river and Mount Fuji. Each of these images contains culturally loaded symbols and costumes (piñata, kimono, mariachi outfit, etc.) that have been used over time in children's books, cartoons, and other formats. These images perpetuate stereotypes such as Latinos having fiestas all the time and Japanese people wearing traditional dress on a daily basis. Moreover, the use of bunny characters to represent the various cultures dehumanizes people from Japan, France, America, and presumably Mexico. What are the effects of these images on a child's self-esteem? Children interacting with this app will gain erroneous, hackneyed perceptions of cultures that may be different from their own. They will learn that Mexicans wear mariachi outfits and play with piñatas, Americans wear cowboy boots and hang out in the desert, Japanese walk around in kimonos to look at Mount Fuji, and the French don sailor costumes to idly gaze at the Eiffel Tower. If children are from any of the cultures represented, they may be confused by the depictions of their culture and wonder if something is wrong with them because they doesn't look like the representation in the app. Alternatively, if children are not from a particular culture described, then they will learn stereotyped information about their classmates or peers from Mexico, Japan, France, or the United States.

Librarians can evaluate the creators of the app to discern their background and purpose. They are then left scratching their heads, wondering why an American author in 2011 takes a tourist approach to cultures when research has shown that this is not the appropriate way to introduce children to cultural diversity and build bridges of cross-cultural understanding. A professional review of the app can be found on the Teachers with Apps website:　http://teacherswithapps.com/bunny-fun-head-shoulders-knees-and-toes/. Note that the reviewer recommends the app but never addresses portrayals of cultural diversity. The cultural portrayals in the app are equally as important as the functionality and concepts explored because they inform children's understanding of various cultures. As we will discuss later in this chapter, while it is good to consult review sources it is also important to consider the background of the reviewer and to use your own professional judgment and understanding of culturally responsive and authentic media for children.

Description of Diversity in Children's Media

Considering how an app or book introduces the topic of diversity to children is extremely important when choosing materials to use in cultural literacy programs. Materials should present culture and diversity naturally to children. The adage "show, don't tell" is just as applicable to digital apps as

Evaluating a Digital App for Bias

B elow are two examples of using the Council on Interracial Books for Children's (CIBC's) *Ten Quick Ways to Analyze Children's Books for Sexism and Racism.* The first example takes a selected app, applies each of the ten points, and then gives a final verdict. The second example, conducted by one of Naidoo's graduate students in library studies, applies the ten points less formally and demonstrates that some areas of bias evaluation are gray, leaving librarians to discern how best to use a digital app with children to introduce cultural literacy while also addressing any cultural stereotypes. The second evaluation also only addresses points of the CIBC guidelines that are clearly observable.

App Name: Up and Down by Mr. Garamond
Summary: In this interactive storybook app, children follow the lives of two boys, presumably pen pals, as they go through their daily routines of play, school, chores, etc. The split screen shows one child from a Western culture and one child most likely from the Western Sahara doing similar things. Children can read the book or have it read to them in Spanish, French, Arabic, or English. Options to read the book by itself or read the book and play a simultaneous matching game are presented. The matching game encourages users to locate similar objects in the two very different worlds of the main characters. Additional activities include a puzzle and coloring pages.

◊ Check the Illustrations/Images—The illustrations/graphics in the book app sensitively portray two diverse cultures, avoiding the use of tokenism and stereotyped objects. Dual visual narratives are displayed on the screen and each child—the one from a Western culture and the one from the Western Sahara—is depicted as a central character.

◊ Check the Storyline or Narrative Material—Each of the dual visual and textual narratives equally depicts both males and females in active roles. Gender stereotyping is avoided and each culture has the power in their respective narrative.

◊ Look at Character Lifestyles—Socioeconomic bias and Eurocentrism seem to be avoided in each of the narratives. No stereotypical assumptions are made or projected about the child and his family living in the Sahara desert. Nor are they portrayed as being less happy because they do not have the same amenities as the child and family from the Western culture.

◊ Weigh the Relationships Between People—The relationships between the main character and his peers, teacher, and family members are equally and positively depicted in each narrative. The illustrator does an excellent job of showing happy, seemingly well-adjusted characters.

◊ Note the Heroes—No heroes are distinctly present in the narratives.

◊ Consider the Effect on a Child's Self-Image—After interacting with the digital app, children will leave with a sense of respect or at least wonder about the Western Saharan culture that is different from their own. If a child happens to be from the general region depicted in that particular narrative, he or she would not feel bad about the depiction of the culture. No cultural stereotypes are projected.

◊ Consider the Creator's Background—Presumably, all of the creators have experience working either with the refugee camps in the Western Saharan desert or with the Bubisher project (an outreach literacy project that includes a traveling bus of books that visits children living in refugee camps in Western Sahara). As such, they have interacted with the cultures depicted in the app and are aware of Western Saharan culture.

◊ Determine the Creator's Perspective—The creators have a social activist slant, particularly in the information section of the app where they state, "The *Up and Down* project is the outcome of many people's endeavours and vision, the need to bring together worlds that are close sometimes but nearly always far apart, the wish to integrate our little day-to-day adventures into a digital environment—in a nutshell, the result of an inquisitive venture into the world of storytelling. And all of these ideas have linked together in this wonderful project: Bubisher, a Travelling Bus of Books for the Children Living in Western Saharan Refugee Camps." An exterior website linked from the information section of the app informs children that the creators are collecting money from the app to support the Bubisher project and get books to children in the refugee camps.

◊ Watch for Loaded Words—The sparse narrative does not include any loaded words or phrases.

◊ Look at the Copyright Date—The copyright of the app is 2012, which means that the information should be accurate.

Final Verdict: The app would be good to use in a cultural literacy program to promote intercultural connections between Western children and children around the world. The various language options expand the audience for the storybook app and the concept presented will

Figure 6.2 continues on page 132

encourage children to learn more about the character from the Western Saharan desert. Using the matching game while sharing the story will help children see how we are the same, same but different.

Review Conducted by Jamie Naidoo

App Name: Mr. Shingu's Paper Halloween
I picked this app because I was at first a bit troubled by its appearance. The character Mr. Shingu is a very stereotypically portrayed Japanese man—long white chin beard, narrow eyes, etc. Mr. Shingu teaches children how to fold origami, which to me only serves to reinforce a stereotype. As I did more research, however, I found that the creator of this app, Stormcloud Games, collaborated with Japanese origami master Mr. Fumiaki Shingu.

it is for any other media for children. Apps that place heavy emphasis on convincing children that it is okay to be different may not be as successful in fostering cultural competence as apps that highlight the accomplishments and contributions of various cultures to our global society. For instance, Joy Tales's *Tab, the White Bat* follows a young bat whose fur is white rather than dark gray/black like the other bats. Tab feels excluded because of his "skin color" and must be convinced that he is okay even though his skin is a different color from his peers. This colorful app, billed by Joy Tales as "the first story [app] thought up to help children discover and appreciate diversity," includes an interactive storybook with facts about bats, games, and a "doctor's file" that describes how educators and parents can use the book to teach about diversity. The creators of the app should be commended for realizing that young children can learn about the culturally diverse world around them through an interactive digital app. However, the method of introducing this concept is very didactic, and perceptive children will quickly be turned off by the heavy-handed message. A better app to teach about diversity would be *Up and Down* by Mr. Garamond, described in Figure 6.2.

Review Sources for Digital Media

Children's librarians will also want to consult professional review sources when choosing digital media to use in programming. While reviews of digital media such as apps are not as plentiful as reviews of books, more and more trustworthy sources are appearing each year. These sources range from blogs to professional books to online and print review media such

Knowing this, I now find this app choice more appropriate because it allows librarians to raise an interesting question—is the portrayal of Mr. Shingu on the app stereotypical if the real Mr. Shingu was involved with the creation of the app? In another Mr. Shingu app, *Mr. Shingu's Paper Zoo,* the character is shown (as a cartoon, of course) in traditional dress. How do we examine this? Was Mr. Shingu OK with this illustration? As for the functionality, these apps are quite good—children can fold digital origami by touch-screen. However, as for the issue of stereotyping in *Mr. Shingu's Paper Halloween* and *Mr. Shingu's Paper Zoo,* that is still up for debate.

Review Conducted by Robert Bodendorf, MLIS Graduate Student,
University of Alabama

Figure 6.2: Evaluating a Digital App Using the Council on Interracial Books
for Children's 10 Quick Ways to Analyze for Sexism and Racism

as *Library Media Connection, Kirkus,* and *School Library Journal.* Figure 6.3 provides an annotated list of various recommended review sources for children's apps.

As with book reviews, librarians can't always be sure that the reviewer has the cultural competence to fully evaluate apps or other digital media. One reason for this is that it is likely that reviewers of digital media, as with reviewers of print materials, may not be from the cultural group or have deep knowledge of the cultural group's customs, language, traditions, and so on. It would be fantastic if a resource such as *Multicultural Review* still existed, as the journal tended to use vetted, expert reviewers so readers could have faith in assessments of culturally diverse materials. That said, we hope that those reviewing will do their best to accurately evaluate the cultural elements of digital media. An example of a professional app review that does take cultural accuracy into consideration is the *Kirkus* review of *The Dream* by Swipea Kids (https://www.kirkusreviews.com/book-reviews/swipea-kids-app/dream-swipea/). The reviewer observes, "the app promotes clichéd notions of Arab life and incorrect information of key elements" and suggests that librarians "steer clear of this app and seek out a well-researched Arab folktale instead." Indeed, when we examined the app, we also noted stereotyping such as a game that encouraged children to help the character select a "costume" to wear and then proceeded to show a hijab and abayah. Using the word "costume" suggests that the character is trying on a cultural identity rather than experiencing it. Swipea Kids' other app, *The Seed,* which purports to help children explore Chinese cultures, also contains stereotypes, particularly visual ones, and should be avoided.

It is important to keep in mind that an app may not receive a review in the aforementioned review resources. Hundred of children's apps are produced each day and with the limited review sources available, it is conceivable that a really amazing app may never receive a review. Fortunately, the blog Learning in Hand with Tony Vincent (http://learninginhand.com/blog/ways-to-evaluate-educational-apps.html) provides several helpful checklists and toolkits for evaluating educational apps. These checklists can be used to evaluate apps under consideration that may not have been professionally reviewed. At the same time, these checklists can be modified to allow librarians to evaluate the culture content of apps for inclusion in culturally competent programming.

Recommended Apps Lists

Just as recommended lists exist for children's printed material, multiple sources provide yearly top lists of recommended apps for children. These lists range from those created by professional library and education associations to those developed by major children's media review sources. A few of these lists are profiled below:

- ◗ Starting in 2013, the American Association of School Librarians (AASL) has published an annual list of the best children's and youth apps with strong potential for curricular connections that support the association's standards for school librarianship. The AASL Best Apps for Teaching and Learning (www.ala.org/aasl/bestapps) suggests top educational apps that cultivate children's learning in libraries through creativity, active participation, innovation, and collaboration.

- ◗ Little eLit's Pinterest page (http://www.pinterest.com/littleelit/) has an extensive listing of recommended apps for various age groups (toddler, preschool, elementary age, teen) and purposes (storytime, anytime/free play, general youth programming, etc.).

- ◗ Each year *Kirkus* publishes Best Book Apps of the Year lists (https://www.kirkusreviews.com/issue/best-of-2013/section/book-apps/lists/) that highlight the best children's and adult apps divided further into categories according to age. For librarians looking for recommended apps to promote cultural competence, the Best International Apps & E-Books list suggests numerous worthy apps.

◊ While not an annual list of recommended apps, the International Reading Association (IRA) profiles apps for educational use and literacy promotion in the "App a Day" section of their *Reading Today Online* website. Each month (not each day), various IRA members highlight an educational app for teachers or apps that can be used with K–12 students (http://www.reading.org/reading-today/ classroom/apps#.UwkAU_Zsh3b).

Digital Media Awards

Numerous awards are given to high-quality children's books, but only a few awards for digital media and apps currently exist and fewer focus on children's digital media. The most notable of these awards are the BolognaRagazzi Digital Award, the Appy Award, the Kids at Play Interactive (KAPi) Awards, Parents' Choice Awards, Digital Book Awards, ON for Learning Award, and iKids Award.

During a five-year period from 1997 to 2002, the Bologna Children's Book Fair and *Children's Technology Review* collaborated to offer an award for new children's media called the Bologna New Media Prize. In 2012 the prize was updated to include interactive digital media in order to recognize excellence and innovation in global children's digital publishing. At this time the prize was renamed the BolognaRagazzi Digital Award and integrated with the BolognaRagazzi prize for printed books. The annual award, which includes both fiction and nonfiction categories, is freely open to any publisher and developer who have created an app in any language or platform for children ages 2 to 15 years old. According to *Children's Technology Review,* "The annual initiative is a comprehensive worldwide search for the state of the art in design and craftsmanship when it comes to narrative driven children's interactive media" (2014, par. 4). Librarians searching for high-quality children's apps that represent the best of global digital literature will want to consult this award for media to use in library programming. *Being Global,* an interactive book app by SachManya and Little Pickle Press, was one of the 2012 BolognaRagazzi Digital Award finalists. It provides opportunities for children to explore numerous ways in which global children are alike but different. More information, including past winners, is available from the Bologna Book Fair website: http://www. bookfair.bolognafiere.it/en/bolognaragazzi-digital-award/1034.html.

Recommended Review Resources for Children's Apps

Specialized App Review Sources

◊ *APPitic* (http://www.appitic.com/) — Aimed at educators, recommends apps for classroom use, divided by theme and curriculum area. Also includes apps categorized by best apps supporting preschoolers, STEM learning, multiple intelligences, special education classrooms, Bloom's Taxonomy, flipped classrooms, and more.

◊ *Best Apps for Kids* (http://bestappsforkids.com/ — Highlights the good, bad, and ugly of children's apps. Divides apps according to age/grade, device, rating, curriculum use, e-book, and more.

◊ *Children's Technology Review* (http://childrenstech.com/) — Subscription-based review source that includes a wide range of digital media for children in addition to apps.

◊ *Common Sense Media* (https://www.commonsensemedia.org/app-reviews) — Categorizes and reviews various types of digital media. While some of their reviews endorse censoring, they do have helpful information on their website.

◊ *Digital Storytime* (http://digital-storytime.com/) — Categorizes and reviews apps by a variety of topics including language options and also provides

First awarded in 2011 by MediaPost Communications, a media and marketing publishing company based in New York, the annual Appy Awards acknowledge outstanding creativity and excellence in app design and development. Apps can be mobile, social, or Web-based and run on various platforms or devices. Approximately forty categories of apps are recognized each year. Of particular interest to children's librarians and educators and those interested in promoting cultural competence are the following categories: books; education; family/parenting; games: educational/family/kids; and multicultural media. Additional information is available from the Appy Awards website: http://www.mediapost.com/appyawards/.

Initially awarded in January 2009 and jointly sponsored by Living in Digital Times (http://www.livingindigitaltimes.com) and *Children's Technology Review* (https://childrenstech.com/), the Kids at Play Interactive (KAPi) Awards identify high-quality children's digital media and technology products that have exemplified excellence and innovation dur-

interviews and new stories relating to digital media usage with children on the blog Digital Media Diet.

◊ *Little eLit* (http://littleelit.com/app-lists-reviews/)—Includes a list of app review websites, specialized lists of apps, and links to blog posts about app reviewing.

◊ *Teachers with Apps* (http://teacherswithapps.com)—Extensive review website of apps organized according to grade level and a few themes such as holidays, seasons, and special needs. Reviews can be sorted according to Teachers with Apps top picks, noteworthy, and book apps. The website also includes a blog about various aspects of apps with a specific entry on celebrating black history.

General Children's Media Review Sources with App Sections

Kirkus iPad Book Apps—https://www.kirkusreviews.com/book-reviews/ipad/

School Library Journal Touch and Go—http://www.slj.com/category/reviews/apps/touch-and-go/

Horn Book App Review of the Week—http://www.hbook.com/category/choosing-books/app-review-of-the-week/

Publishers Weekly This Week in Children's Apps—http://www.publishersweekly.com/pw/by-topic/digital/Apps/index.html

Figure 6.3: Recommended Review Resources for Children's Apps

ing the previous year. Products considered include video games, music, computer games, apps, toys with interactive features, and websites. An individual who has been a pioneer in the field of children's interactive media is also recognized by the KAPi Awards. Additional information is available at https://childrenstech.com/kapis.

Originally awarded in 1978, the Parents' Choice Awards represent the oldest U.S. nonprofit developed to recognize high-quality children's media. Categories include books, toys, music and storytelling, magazines, software, mobile apps, videogames, television, and websites. The awards for mobile apps began in 2010 and the Parent's Choice also features apps of the week. More information is available at http://www.parents-choice.org/allawards.cfm.

Since January 2011 *Digital Book World* has annually awarded the Digital Book Awards, which recognize innovation, creativity, and excellence in digital book publishing. More than fifteen categories of awards are given to e-books, apps, and transmedia for both children and adults. Criteria for the awards are innovation, design, usability, content, consistency, and excellence. Additional information including past winners is available at http://www.digitalbookworld.com/the-digital-book-awards/.

Awarded for the first time in 2013, Common Sense Media's ON for Learning Award goes to the best children's digital media that effectively combine fun and learning. Apps, websites, and games given a top "ON" rating by Common Sense Media are eligible for the honor. Awards are given in the following age categories: preschoolers (2-4), little kids (5-7), big kids (8-9), tweens (10-12), and teens (13 and up). For more information visit http://www.commonsensemedia.org/lists/2013-on-for-learning-award-winners.

In February 2013 Kidscreen awarded the first annual iKids Awards for the best digital media for preschoolers and kids ages six and up. Categories are Best Website, Best Learning App, Best Game App, Best Web/App Series, Best eBook, Best Console Video Game, Best Handheld Video Game, and Best Streaming Video Platform. Kidscreen also gives awards to high-quality children's broadcasting. Additional information can be found at http://ikidsawards.kidscreen.com/.

Note: Librarians interested in awards and book lists for culturally diverse children's books should consult the Bibliography for more information.

Outside Cultural Influences

Caregivers, librarians, and educators may also influence the way a child experiences an app. Adults may have biases and assumptions about different cultures that are projected onto the child when they encourage or discourage the use of particular apps. A bookseller writing for the Lee & Low blog observed that it was often adults who discouraged their young white children from reading books depicting non-white people. These kinds of behaviors may discourage an otherwise open-minded child from exploring in print and digital media cultures that are different from his or her own.

It also follows that an adult's lack of familiarity with particular cultures may make them hesitant to introduce a particular book or app to children. Because adults may be more familiar with popular, white or non-raced characters from movies such as *Cinderella* or *Cars,* they may feel more comfortable introducing related digital media to their children. If they are less familiar with, say, Native American culture, they may be unwilling to introduce children to an app that engages more directly with authentic Native American culture. This may arise out of fear that young people will be introduced to stereotypical images of Native Americans, but most often it is an internalized, unspoken discomfort with the "other" in society.

The solution then is for adults to increase their own cultural competence through education, reading, attending workshops, or other means. They must be open-minded about their own biases and how these may influence the children in their care. For cultural competence to be promoted in cultural literacy programs, children's librarians need to make a concerted effort to include print and digital media about diverse cultures and provide a forum for discussing diversity and making cross-cultural connections. Using well-chosen, culturally responsive books, apps, and other digital media in such a forum certainly lays the foundation for building bridges of understanding among children, caregivers, and librarians. Jella Lepman would be proud!

References

Bircher, Katie. (February 28, 2012). "What Makes a Good Picture Book App?" *Horn Book*. Accessed February 22, 2014, at http://www.hbook.com/2012/02/using-books/what-makes-a-good-picture-book-app.

Children's Technology Review. (2014). BolognaRagazzi Digital Award. Accessed February 10, 2014, at http://childrenstech.com/bolognaragazzidigital.

Council on Interracial Books for Children. *Ten Quick Ways to Analyze Children's Books for Sexism and Racism*. New York: Council on Interracial Books for Children, 1980.

Falloon, Garry. "Young Students Using iPads: App Design and Content Influences on Their Learning Pathways." *Computers & Education* 68 (2013): 505-521.

Gardner, Howard, and Katie Davis. *The App Generation: How Today's Youth Navigate Identity, Intimacy, and Imagination in a Digital World*. New Haven, CT: Yale University Press, 2013.

Home, Anna. (1995). *Charter for Children's Television*. First World Summit on Children and Television. Accessed February 23, 2014, at http://www.wsmcf.com/charters/charter.htm.

Ito, Mizuko, Cathy Davidson, Henry Jenkins, Carol Lee, Michael Eisenberg, and Joanne Weiss. "Foreword." In *Youth, Identity, and Digital Media.* Ed. by David Buckingham (pp. vii–ix). The John D. and Catherine T. MacArthur Foundation Series on Digital Media and Learning. Cambridge, MA: MIT Press, 2008. Accessed February 22, 2014, at https://mitpress.mit.edu/sites/default/files/titles/free_download/9780262524834_Youth_Identity_and_Digital_Media.pdf.

Kucirkova, Natalia, David Messer, Kieron Sheehy, and Carmen Fernández Panadero. "Children's Engagement with Educational iPad Apps: Insights from a Spanish Classroom." *Computers & Education* 71 (2014): 175-184.

Larrick, Nancy. "The All-White World of Children's Books," *Saturday Review* (September 11, 1965): 63-65.

Lepman, Jella. *A Bridge of Children's Books: The Inspiring Autobiography of a Remarkable Woman.* Dublin: The O'Brien Press, 2002. (Originally published in German in 1964 by Fischer as *Die Kinderbuchbrücke.*)

Nemeth, Karen. (March 6, 2012). "Designing a Rubric for Preschool Bilingual Apps." *Early Childhood Technology Network.* Accessed December 19, 2013, at http://www.ecetech.net/blog/dll/designing-a-rubric-for-preschool-bilingual-apps-by-karen-nemeth/.

Simon, Fran, and Karen Nemeth. *Digital Decisions: Choosing the Right Technology Tools for Early Childhood Education.* Lewisville, NC: Gryphon House, 2012.

◊ Chapter 7

Recommended Digital Media for Promoting Cultural Competence

Like all types of technology, apps and digital media come and go as more robust and dynamic applications and devices appear. The best digital media today is tomorrow's dinosaur. While many attempts have been made to curate existing apps, librarians will never be able to capture all the children's apps available at a given time. The important thing is for children's and school librarians to subscribe to the idea that apps hold great potential for promoting multiple literacies and cultural competence. Apps are the tools by which librarians help children learn information and develop cultural understanding. Throughout this chapter, librarians will encounter various recommended apps for use in cultural literacy programs to connect with digital natives. While a particular recommended app might not be available in the future for use in a children's program, librarians have the skills to locate a comparable app using review sources that will accomplish the same goal.

Digital media in this chapter include recommended apps, e-books, online games, and web resources that can be used to promote cultural competence and global understanding in children's library programs or individual family explorations. Each entry includes a brief description of the resource and enough information to locate it using your chosen platform or device. In some instances, pairings of recommended print books have been provided to help make programming connections. Since web URLs change continuously, only URLs for specific comprehensive websites are provided. Apps can be located in Google Play, iTunes, or stores supporting specialized platforms. Web resources are not meant to represent the vast array of children's websites covering multicultural themes or topics. Rather, they provide opportunities to help children make global connections.

Apps

ABC Music. Peapod Labs LLC. (App, Multicultural)—Children are invited on an interactive musical exploration to learn about various instruments from around the world. Includes videos of instruments being played as well as cartoon characters that help children sound out letters. Available in Spanish and English. Pair with: *Wee Sing Around the World* audiobook by Pamela Conn Beall and Susan Hagen Nipp (Price Stern Sloan, 2006), or with *Music Everywhere!* by Maya Ajmera, Elise Hofer Derstine, and Cynthia Pon (Charlesbridge, 2014).

The Amazing Train. PlaneTree Family Productions. (App, Indian)—All aboard for an out-of-this-world adventure! This storybook app follows four children from Udaipur, India, as they board the Magnificent Traveling Palace train for a magical adventure that includes stellar 3-D graphics, games, and an Indian dessert recipe. Pair with: *Going to School in India* by Lisa Heydlauff, Nitin Upadyhe, and Global Fund for Children (Charlesbridge, 2005).

Anompa: Chickasaw Language Basic. Thornton Media. (App, Native American, Chickasaw)—Upper elementary children will find this interactive educational app useful as they learn the basic alphabet and phrases from the Chickasaw language as well as information about the culture. Includes songs as well as two videos of children speaking Chickasaw. Thornton Media, a Native American-owned app development company, offers several other Native American language-learning apps. Pair with: *Chikasha Stories: Shared Spirit* (Vol. 1) by Glenda Galvan, illus. by Jeannie Barbour (Chickasaw Press, 2011).

Axel's Chain Reaction. Laura Allison Pomenta Badolato. (App, Differently Able)—This highly engaging storybook app includes 3-D animation, music, and required interactivity to propel the narrative. Children are introduced to Axel, a neuro-divergent kid (autism, Tourette's, etc.), who enjoys making things but doesn't fit in. He decides to create a kinetic sculpture for a class project to win everyone's admiration. The app ties into Common Core Standards and STEM/STEAM learning and includes step-by-step instructions for making kinetic sculptures, hands-on games, and information about kinetic artists. Pair with: *My Brother Charlie* by Holly Robinson Peete and Ryan Elizabeth Peete, illus. by Shane Evans (Scholastic, 2010).

Barefoot World Atlas. Touch Press. (App, Multicultural)—With this interactive educational app, children can explore various cultures of the world learning geographical and cultural facts as well as exploring languages, art, and more. Includes games as well as 3-D graphics. Available in English, French, Spanish, Catalan, Japanese, and German. Pair with: *My Librarian Is a Camel: How Books Are Brought to Children Around the World* by Margriet Ruurs (Boyds Mills Press, 2005).

Being Global. SachManya LLC and Little Pickle Press. (App, Multicultural)—Based on *What Does It Mean to Be Global?* by Rana DiOrio, this multiple award-winning story app encourages children to actively explore the concept of being global. In addition to the story, the interactive app includes opportunities to journal and draw pictures, sing-along, and color. Children learn facts about other countries such as foods, languages, and climate. The possibilities for extensions into a cultural literacy program are expansive. Available in English and Spanish. Pair with: *This Child, Every Child: A Book About the World's Children* by David J. Smith, illus. by Shelagh Armstrong (Kids Can Press, 2011).

Bramble Berry Tales: The Great Sasquatch. Loud Crow Interactive. (App, First Nations, Canadian, Stó:l_)—Thomas and his younger sister are back in this second storybook app in the Bramble Berry Tales. This time their grandfather tells them a story about the great Sasquatch, meant to teach them the importance of not judging someone based on outward appearances. Three-dimensional animation and an interactive interface feature in the Stó:l_ Nation tale, which is available in English, French, Spanish, and Halq'eméylem. Pair with: *The Kids Book of Aboriginal Peoples in Canada* by Diane Silvey, illus. by John Mantha (Kids Can Press, 2012).

Bramble Berry Tales: The Story of Kalkalilh. Loud Crow Interactive. (App, First Nations, Canadian, Squamish)—Lily and her older brother Thomas learn about the dangers of accepting treats from strangers in this interactive, Squamish cautionary tale. Including animations and 3-D graphics, this storybook app is the first in series of First Nations stories by Loud Crow Interactive. Available in Squamish, English, Spanish, and French. Pair with children's titles found at the Squamish Lil'wat Cultural Centre: http://www.shop. slcc.ca/books/childrens.

But That Won't Wake Me Up. Adarna House. (App, Filipino)—Maya is worried that she'll oversleep the following morning. The young girl's mother comforts her fears by supplying a list of ways she'll wake her up. The interactive app includes vibrant illustrations and would work well in a storytime devoted to bedtime. Available in English and Filipino. Pair with: *It's Bedtime, Cucuy/A La Cama, Cucuy* by Claudia Galindo, illus. by Jonathan Coombs (Piñata Books, 2008), or with *Ladder to the Moon* by Maya Soetoro-Ng, illus. by Yuyi Morales (Candlewick, 2011).

Curly Hair, Straight Hair. 33 Loretta Kids' Books. (App, Multicultural)—Children can learn both Spanish and English words for various objects and phrases in this bilingual interactive app that follows two girls, one Black and one presumably Caucasian, as they go through daily rituals: riding the bus, taking a bath, going to school, etc. The rhythmic text, which introduces hair differences, could be paired with any number of children's books that explore the topic of hair. Pair with: *I Love My Hair!* by Natasha Anastasia Tarpley, illus. by E. B. Lewis (Little, Brown, 1998), or with *Dalia's Wondrous Hair / El maravilloso cabello de Dalia* by Laura Lacámara (Piñata Books, 2014).

A Day in the Market. Adarna House. (App, Filipino)—Off to market we go with this picture-book app based on the Philippine National Children's Book Award-winning picture book *Araw sa Palengke* by May Tobias-Papa and Isabel Roxas. Beautiful illustrations and graphics invite children into this interactive app that follows a young girl as she explores a market for the first time. Text is available in Filipino and English and various activities and games are included. Available in Filipino and English. Pair with: *Market Day: A Story Told with Folk Art* by Lois Ehlert (Harcourt, 2000), or with *To Market, to Market* by Nikki McClure (Abrams, 2011).

Drum Circle Kids. SPYE Studio, LLC. (App, Multicultural)—A music-oriented app that introduces children to different types of drum music from various cultures around the world: the American Trap Set, Caribbean Steel Pan, Chinese Drum, Cuban Conga, and the West African Djembe. Children learn drum facts and sounds in this interactive app, which also includes a game. Pair with: *Drum, Chavi, Drum!/¡Toca, Chavi, toca!* by Mayra Lazara Dole, illus. by Tonel (Children's Book Press, 2003).

Fam Bam: Got to Have Music. See Here Studios LLC. (App, African American)—Featuring singer Brandy Norwood and her family, this interactive storybook app uses a close-knit African American family and their talking dog to teach children about various types of music. Pair with: *Hip Hop Speaks to Children with CD: A Celebration of Poetry with a Beat* by Nikki Giovanni (Sourcebooks, 2008).

Fatima Al Fihria, Story of the Founder of Al Qarawiyin. Masarat App. (App, Muslim)—In this picture-book biography app, elementary children are introduced to Fatima Al Fihria, a woman who established the University of Al Qarawiyin in Morocco in 859. Bright illustrations accompany a visual and audio narrative that can be read in English, French, or Arabic. Includes a puzzle and coloring pages. Pair with: *Extraordinary Women from the Muslim World* by Natalie Maydell and Sep Riahi, illus. by Heba Amin (Global Content Publishing, 2008), or with *A Library for Juana: The World of Sor Juana Ines* by Pat Mora, illus. by Beatriz Vidal (Knopf, 2002).

Frida's World. Gramercy Consultants. (App, Mexican)—Middle elementary children are introduced to Frida Kahlo in this slightly interactive picture-book app biography. Whimsical illustrations and the background folk music accompany the bilingual Spanish-English narrative options and a coloring book. Pair with picture-book biographies about Frida such as *Frida* by Jonah Winter, illus. by Ana Juan (Arthur A. Levine, 2002), or with *Me, Frida* by Amy Novesky, illus. by David Diaz (Abrams, 2010).

Geoff and His Two Dads: Tomato Trouble. Wompi Studios. (App, LGBTQ)—In this picture-book app, Geoff, a Jack Russell terrier who lives in New South Wales, Australia, with his two dads, gets into a muddy mess involving tomatoes and a load of once-clean laundry. Interactivity features are minimal with the ability only to adjust sounds, narration, music, and page turns. While not the most engaging story for a group reading, this e-book would work well shared one-on-one with a child.

Get Water! Decode Global. (App, Indian)—Created for upper elementary children and young adults, this interactive educational gaming app encourages users to help a girl from India collect water for her village quickly so she can get back to school. The social justice message can lead to many extensions and educators will appreciate the detailed packet of science activities available on the developer's website, http://getwatergame.com/. Pair with: *A Long Walk to Water: Based on a True Story* by Linda Sue Park (Clarion, 2010), or with *Boys Without Names* by Kashmira Sheth (HarperCollins, 2010).

Henrietta Is Hungry. PicPocket Books. (App, Multicultural)—A young girl is hungry and goes on a global adventure to find something that will satisfy her appetite. With its focus on food, this interactive app is borderline didactic but might provide a springboard for discussing global cultures, particularly if a librarian helps children find other stories and informational books about the cultures mentioned.

It's a Small World. Disney. (App, Multicultural)—Designed for the youngest children, this interactive story app depicts a host of children from all around the world. The narrative is the original Disney song and the only cultural aspects are the illustrations. Some of the illustrations depict children in traditional "costumes" and others are more contemporary. This could create a forum for discussing visual representations of cultures, particularly with upper elementary children. However, librarians might want to consider whether these stereotypical images are appropriate for younger children. The app includes the ability to select one of nine different languages for the sing-along portion.

Kids of the Ummah: Exploring the Global Muslim Community. Magnicode, Inc. (App, Muslim)—Created by Peter Gould, this interactive educational storybook app introduces young readers to the global diversity within the Muslim culture through 26 children. The charming app includes games, puzzles, a story, and coloring sheets. A lengthy party kit with various activities is also available at http://www.kidsoftheummah.com/. Forthcoming apps about Muslim cultures for multiple age groups include: Salam Sisters, Dinars and Dynasties, Amina's Kitchen, and NoorQuest: Muslim Space Kids. Pair with: *Deep in the Sahara* by Kelly Cunnane, illus. by Hoda Hadadi (Schwartz & Wade, 2013), or with *Golden Domes and Silver Lanterns: A Muslim Book of Colors* by Hena Khan, illus. by Mehrdokht Amini (Chronicle Books, 2012).

Let's Bake Challah! A Jewish Baking App. G-dcast. (App, Jewish)—Want to bake challah bread but not get your hands dirty? This interactive app allows children to create and "bake" their own challah for sharing. The app would be a great accompaniment to books about Jewish culture or a storytime about breads from around the world. Pair with: *This Is the Challah* by Sue Hepker, illus. by Amy Wummer (Behrman House, 2012), or with *It's Challah Time!* by Latifa Berry Kropf, illus. by Tod Cohen (Kar-Ben, 2002).

Let's Get Ready for Passover! G-dcast. (App, Jewish)—In this interactive gaming app children learn about the various preparations involved in getting the house ready for Passover. Also, includes the opportunity to "bake" food.

Little Dead Riding Hood. itBook (App)—From the outset, the word "dead" in the title should alert librarians that this interactive story app is not your grandmother's version of the darling girl with the little red hood. In this fractured fairy tale, granny ends up dead—accidentally poisoned by her decomposing granddaughter who has been sent to the land of the living to execute a plan cooked up by her evil and equally dead parents. A creepy narrator, dark illustrations, 3-D animations, and spooky music move this undead story along. Available in English and Spanish, the app will hold great appeal for upper elementary children and young adults and would be great used in a library program relating to the Day of the Dead.

Lucha Libre USA: Make Your Own Masked Warrior. Night & Day Studios, Inc. (App, Latino, Mexican)—Who wouldn't want to become a masked luchador and dream of wrestling matches?! This simple app allows users to snap photos of friends, pets, themselves, etc., and then develop their own luchador mask and corresponding wrestling poster. The app is a perfect companion to books exploring Mexican lucha libre wrestling. Pair with: *Lucha Libre: The Man in the Silver Mask* by Xavier Garza (Cinco Punto Press, 2002), or with *Niño Wrestles the World* by Yuyi Morales (Roaring Brook Press, 2013).

Magikid Nian. Magikid. (App, Chinese)—Celebrate Chinese New Year with songs, games, and stories through this interactive gaming and educational app that teaches children about various elements of Chinese culture relating to Chinese New Year. Available in Chinese and English. Pair with: *Happy, Happy Chinese New Year!* by Demi (Crown Books, 2003), or with *Bringing in the New Year* by Grace Lin (Random House, 2008).

Matisyahu's 'Happy Hanukkah' Jam-Along. Mibblio. (App, Jewish)—Bright, cheerful illustrations abound in this interactive musical app that allows children to play various musical instruments as they learn a song in celebration of Hanukkah.

My Grandma Reads Me Books. GloyeonBooks. (App, Korean)—Celebrate intergenerational bonds in this heartwarming, soothing picture-book app about a young Korean girl, Min-jeong, who reads to her grandmother every night over the phone because her Grandma can't read. As a surprise to the family, Grandma learns to read and now reads to her granddaughter each night. Music and interactive features allow children to record their own voices, play music and games, and color accompanying soft oil illustrations. Pair with: *The Have a Good Day Café* by Frances Park and Ginger Park, illus. by Katherine Potter (Lee & Low Books, 2008), or with *Dear Juno* by Soyung Pak, illus. by Susan Kathleen Hartung (Penguin Puffin, 1999).

Navajo Toddler. Isreal Shortman. (App, Native American, Navajo)—In this interactive educational app, young children are introduced to basic Navajo words such as numbers, foods, colors, and animals. As children participate in multiple games and activities, auditory and visual cues help them in their language acquisition. Pair with: *Colors of the Navajo* by Emily Abbink, illus. by Janice Porter (Carolrhoda Books, 1998).

Neomad Interactive Comic. BighART. (App, Aboriginal, Australian)—Set in the Western Australia desert and in outer space, this interactive graphic novel app offers middle elementary school students a glimpse into contemporary oral and written storytelling created by their peers in Australia. The graphic novel format interspersed with videos of the child creators will appeal to the target audience and likely attract reluctant readers with its fresh style. Pair with: *Rift Breaker* by Tristan Michael Savage (Magabala Books, 2014), or with other middle reader or young adult titles on contemporary Australian aboriginals at www.magabala.com/.

One Globe Kids: Children's Stories from Around the World. Round by Design. (App, Multicultural)—Grab your virtual passports and visit Haiti, the Netherlands, Indonesia, New York City, and Burundi. In this interactive app, children connect to "friends" in other parts of the world to hear a story, take a look around, and learn some cool facts along the way. The app is designed to make younger children think they are really using a social network to connect with other children; in actuality children are listening to prerecorded stories from other children. The app includes one friend for free (Haiti) and children must purchase more friends to explore other countries. The app has multiple possibilities for library programming and is narrated in English, French, and Dutch. Pair with: *Off to Class: Incredible and Unusual Schools Around the World* by Susan Hughes (Owlkids Books, 2011).

Papa's Boy. Tapisodes Ltd. (App, LGBTQ)—A cross between Kimberly Bradley's *Ballerino Nate* and Harvey Fierstein's *The Sissy Duckling*, this e-book app follows a boy mouse who would much rather be performing his ballet than practicing the boxing skills his dad insists he learns. When a cat traps the mouse's father, it is the twirling, tutu-swathed boy mouse who saves the day. Although the app offers little beyond music and narration, it does offer an opportunity to talk about gender-variance and the importance of being true to one's self. It would also work in a subversive storytime inclusive of lesbian, gay, bisexual, transgender, and queer (LGBTQ) families. Pair with: *Jose! Born to Dance: The Story of Jose Limon* by Susanna Reich, illus. by Raúl Colón (Simon & Schuster, 2005), or with *Dogs Don't Do Ballet* by Anna Kemp, illus. by Sara Ogilvie (Simon & Schuster, 2010).

Los Pollitos. Cantos. (App, Latino)—Perfect for bilingual Spanish-English storytimes, this musical app teaches young children the popular Latin American song "Los Pollitos *Dicen*/Baby Chicks Sing." Functionality includes several different options of singers in English and Spanish. Multiple hot spots encourage children to make each chick sing "pío, pío, pío" and to facilitate interactions between the mother hen and her babies. Pair with: *Los Pollitos Dicen / The Baby Chicks Sing* by Nancy Abraham Hall and Jill Syverson-Stork, illus. by Kay Chorao (Little Brown, 1994), or with *¡Pío Peep!: Traditional Spanish Nursery Rhymes* by Alma Flor Ada and F. Isabel Campoy, illus. by Vivi Escriva (HarperCollins/Rayo, 2003).

Rosita y Conchita: A Peek 'n Play Story App. Mobad Games. (App, Latino, Mexican)—Available in English and Spanish, this heartwarming storybook app follows two sisters, Rosita and Conchita, separated by death. Each year they are reunited during the Day of the Dead celebration. Unfortunately, this year Rosita is running late and needs the readers' help to see her sister before midnight. Three-D graphics grab children's attention along with multiple hot spots (points for children to touch on the screen that will cause an action to occur), a drawing game, cooking recipe, and more. Pair with other books about Day of the Dead celebrations in various Latin American countries to compare and contrast the differences among cultures. Suggested titles: *Felipa and the Day of the Dead* by Birte Müller (North South Books, 2004) (set in Peru). And *Barrilete: A Kite for the Day of the Dead* by Elisa Amado, illus. by Joya Hairs (Groundwood Books, 1999) (set in Guatemala).

Stack the Countries. Freecloud Design, Inc. (App, Multicultural)— Global exploration is fun and engaging in this interactive gaming app that encourages children to learn about countries around the world and to pick up fast facts. This would be a great app to pair with informational books on specific countries or fictional books depicting children from some of the countries encountered. Pair with titles from International Board on Books for Young People's (IBBY's) Books for Africa, Books from Africa project: http://www.ibby.org/index.php?id=553. Or with titles from the International Children's Digital Library: http://en.childrenslibrary.org/.

Touchable Earth [Educational Version]. Touchable Earth. (App, Multicultural)—Billed as the "first dedicated Global Citizenship app for kids," this interactive educational app allows children to click various hot spots on the world map to view videos from real children (ages 7 to 12) who describe their family, home, school, clothing, games, etc. Subtitles are included for videos not recorded in English. Users must usually purchase stories to learn about the children living in each country, but the educational version has removed the in-app purchase option and included the countries Nepal, India, South Africa, Romania, Iraqi Kurdistan, and China in the standard purchase price. Pair with: *Mimi's Village: And How Basic Health Care Transformed It* by Katie Smith Milway, illus. by Eugenie Fernandes (Kids Can Press, 2012).

Up and Down. Mr. Garamond. (App, Western and African)—In this interactive storybook app, children follow the lives of two boys, presumably pen pals, as they go through their daily routines of play, school, chores, etc. The split screen shows one child from Western culture and one child most likely from the Western Sahara doing similar things. Children can read the book or have it read to them in Spanish, French, Arabic, or English. Options to read the book by itself or read the book and play a simultaneous matching game are presented. The matching game encourages users to locate similar objects in the two very different worlds of the main characters.

Additional activities include a puzzle and coloring pages. Pair with: *Same, Same But Different* by Jenny Sue Kostecki-Shaw (Henry Holt, 2011).

Wake Up World: An Interactive Rosh Hashanah Book for the Jewish New Year. G-dcast. (App, Jewish) — Young children can learn a little about the Rosh Hashanah, the Jewish New Year, in this interactive app that follows a main character as the child wakes up the world by blowing the shofar to prepare for the celebration. Functionality includes the ability to change the main character to a boy or a girl and blow the shofar using your device's microphone. Available in Hebrew and English. Pair with: *The Secret Shofar of Barcelona* by Jacqueline Dembar Greene, illus. by Douglas Chayka (Kar-Ben, 2009), or with *Sammy Spider's First Rosh Hashanah* by Sylvia Rouss, illus. by Katherine Janus Kahn (Kar-Ben, 1996).

Walter's Flying Bus. Chosen and Dearly Loved LLC. (App, Ugandan, Differently Able) — Based on real children in a special needs orphanage in Uganda, this interactive storybook app describes the journey of Walter and his friends as they find a broken-down bus, breathe new life into it, and follow his dream of being a bus driver. Includes original music, mini-documentaries of the featured children, and artwork created by the children. Available in English, Spanish, and Luganda. Pair with: *Beatrice's Goat* by Page McBrier, illus. by Lori Lohstoeter (Atheneum Books for Young Readers, 2001).

E-Books and E-Book Platforms

Bookboard (http://bookboard.com/) — A subscription-based digital picture-book platform that allows users to purchase various levelized e-books chosen by a trained children's librarian. The platform launches as an app and a selection of books is accessible through a monthly subscription, rather than on the book-by-book basis common to such platforms as Reading Rainbow and TumbleBooks. Books cover a variety of topics, including global titles such as *May All Children (Music Together(r) Singalong Storybook)* by Kenneth K. Guilmartin and Kristina Swarner.

Cora Cooks Pancit. Shen Books. (E-book, Filipino) — Using the KiteReaders platform, this is the e-book version of the picture book of the same title created by Dorina K. Lazo Gilmore and Kristi Valiant. Bright, expressive illustrations are inviting to readers as they follow a young Filipino girl as she cooks her favorite dish—pancit. Although the e-book has limited functionality, the story is culturally authentic and would be great to use in storytime, particularly with cooking activities. Could be paired with *A Day in the Market* app.

Fundels (http://www.fundels.com/en_UK/)—A digital picture-book platform that allows users to purchase interactive, global picture books from a growing library of high-quality Dutch and Flemish children's books. The platform can be loaded on a computer or mobile device.

Good Fortune in a Wrapping Cloth. Shen's Books. (E-book, Korean)—Using the KiteReaders platform, this is the e-book version of the picture book of the same title created by Joan Schoettler and Jessica Lanan. Beautifully rendered watercolor illustrations accompany a historical narrative that follows a young Korean girl, Ji-su, as she tries to make the best *bojagi*, or wrapping cloths, for the royal family so she can be reunited with her mother, a seamstress for the family. Functionality is limited to narration but the engaging tale could be displayed using a projection system during storytime.

The Great Voyages of Zheng He. Shen's Books. (E-book, Chinese)—Using the KiteReaders platform, this is the e-book version of the picture book of the same title created by Demi. Vivid, detailed illustrations accompany an engaging, informative narrative about one of China's powerful military leaders, Zheng He. The e-book's functionality is limited but the culturally authentic story could be shared using a projection system.

Maneki Neko: The Tale of the Beckoning Cat. Shen's Books. (E-book, Japanese)—Using the KiteReaders platform, this is the e-book version of the picture book created by Susan Lendroth and Kathryn Otoshi. Striking illustrations accompany this retelling of the Japanese legend of the beckoning cat Maneki Neko. Functionality is limited to narration but the engaging tale could be displayed using a projection system during storytime.

Milly Molly Books. Kiwa Media. (E-book, European New Zealanders, Maori—Indigenous Polynesian people of New Zealand)—Using the Kiwa Media platform, the Milly Molly e-books originate from the long-standing New Zealand early-reader series that promotes intercultural acceptance and understanding. Originally the print books were created to help with the tension between European New Zealanders and the indigenous Maori people of New Zealand. The global message of cross-cultural friendship makes this extensive series perfect for library collections. Available in English, Italian, Arabic, Maori, and Spanish.

Reading Rainbow: Read Along Children's Books. Reading Rainbow. (http://www.readingrainbow.com/)—This subscription-based e-book library offers hundred of books and video clips on a variety of topics using the Reading Rainbow platform. Some vintage episodes are included but new content is added on a regular basis. The company maintains its commitment to diversity by including multicultural children's books and topics in the mix.

Selvakumar Knew Better. Shen's Books. (E-book, Indian)—Using the KiteReaders platform, this is the e-book version of the picture book of the same title created by Virginia Kroll and Xiaojun Li. Based on a true story, the narrative describes how a young boy in India is saved from a tsunami by his dog. The e-book has limited functionality aside from narration but the culturally authentic story could spark further exploration into tsunamis or Indian culture.

Story Cove: A World of Stories (http://www.storycove.com/)—A subscription-based e-book library that includes "folktalkes from around the globe." Stories feature some animation as well as narration and highlighting of words as they are read. The folktales represented cover many global cultures but some of the storylines and illustrations include stereotypes. Librarians would need to use the Council on Interracial Books for Children's guidelines to evaluate these e-books on a case-by-case basis to find hidden gems.

TumbleBooks (http://www.tumblebooks.com/)—This subscription-based ebook library includes digital picture books and levelized readers with sounds and narration but offers little interactivity. The books could be displayed using an LCD projector and screen, allowing all the children in storytime to see the images. Also available as an app with each book purchased separately. Titles that feature cultural diversity include *The Best Mariachi Band in the World* by J. D. Smith (Latino), *I Love Saturday y domingos* by Alma Flor Ada (Latino, bicultural), *Bintou's Braids* by Sylvianne Diouf (West African), *Just Like Josh Gibson* by Angela Johnson (African American), *A Perfect Season of Dreaming* by Benjamin Alire Sáenz (Latino), *Bebé Goes Shopping* by Susan Middleton Elya (Hispanic), *A Chanukah Noel* by Sharon Jennings (French, Jewish), *Belle of Batoche* by Jacqueline Guest (Métis First Nation People, Canadian),

Fatty Legs by Christy Jordan-Fenton and Margaret Pokiak-Fenton (Inuvialuit/Western Canadian Inuit), and *Hannah Is My Name* by Belle Yang (Taiwanese).

We Give Books (www.wegivebooks.org)—A free Web-based collection of picture-book, nonfiction, and early chapter e-books developed by the Penguin Group and the Pearson Foundation. The static books don't contain any narration or animation but could be shared with children using a projection system. Some titles featuring cultural diversity include *Old Mikamba Had a Farm* by Rachel Isadora (African), *Before You Were Here, Mi Amor* by Samantha Vamos (Latino), *Welcome to China* by DK Readers (Chinese), *Back of the Bus* by Aaron Reynolds (African American), and *The Hallelujah Flight* by Phil Bildner (African American).

Online Games

Ayiti: The Cost of Life (http://ayiti.globalkids.org/game/)—Available in both online and mobile app formats, this engaging game, created by Global Kids, challenges upper elementary children, young adults, and adults to help a Haitian family survive over a period of time. The game educates users about the intricacy of the global issues facing impoverished people in developing countries.

Free Rice (http://freerice.com/)—A non-profit website supporting the United Nations World Food Programme. The global awareness game donates free food to starving families based on online participation.

Games for Change (http://www.gamesforchange.org/)—This site provides a list of games for a variety of ages that deal with social issues around the world. All games are not appropriate for children; librarians will want to review them on a game-by-game basis.

Half the Sky Movement (http://www.halftheskymovement.org/)—Web-based games and apps explore health, gender equality, and other important global social issues. All games are not appropriate for children; librarians will want to review them on a game-by-game basis.

Peace Corp for Kids (http://www.peacecorps.gov/kids/)—Recommended by the Best Websites for Kids committee of the Association for Library Service to Children (a division of the American Library Association), this online game teaches elementary children about social activism and introduces them to various cultures around the world.

Purposeful Games for Social Change (http://purposefulgames.info/)— This site provides a list of online games collected by the MIT Game Lab that teach children, teens, and adults about global and social issues facing our world. All games are not appropriate for children; librarians will want to review them on a game-by-game basis.

Web Resources

ePals (http://www.epals.com/#!/global-community/)—ePals is a global educational network that helps children connect for global collaborations centered around literacy. It is a great resource for mock book award and literature discussions with their In2books program and allows users to connect and collaborate on various projects through its GlobalCommunity program.

G-dcast: Meaningful Jewish Screentime (http://www.g-dcast.com/)— With almost 100 cartoon-free podcasts for children, tweens, and young adults, this website provides opportunities to explore various aspects of the Jewish religion. The short clips can serve as great discussion starters or accompany apps or books about Jewish culture.

Global Kids Online Leadership Program by Global Kids, Inc. (http://www.olpglobalkids.org)—An educational program for older children and teens promoting the use of digital media to foster global awareness, digital literacy, and social activism. Digital media include video games, virtual worlds, social media, and other forms of participatory media.

Kid World Citizen (http://kidworldcitizen.org/)—Developed by a classroom teacher dedicated to promoting cultural awareness, this site features games, details of international celebrations, recipes, cultural art projects, reviews of global children's literature, and many hands-on activities.

Mama Lisa's World: International Music and Culture (http://www.mamalisa.com/)—Contains lyrics to children's songs and rhymes from around the world in a variety of languages. Apps with audio versions of the songs are available to download from the app store and organized by language.

National Geographic Kids (http://kids.nationalgeographic.com/kids/)—
This well-respected name in education offers a website filled with
games, activities, and new stories about cultures around the world.

Bibliography

A listing of awards, publishers, and professional resources relating to cultural diversity in children's programming, diversity in media for children, and digital media usage with children.

Selected Professional Books

Alexander, Lina B., and Nahyun Kwon. 2010. *Multicultural Programs for Tweens and Teens.* Chicago, IL: American Library Association.

Asamen, Joy Keiko, Mesha L. Ellis, and Gordon L. Berry. 2008. *The SAGE Handbook of Child Development, Multiculturalism, and Media.* Thousand Oaks, CA: SAGE.

Bishop, Rudine Sims. 2007. *Free Within Ourselves: The Development of African American Children's Literature.* Westport, CT: Greenwood Press.

Botelho, Maria José, and Masha Kabakow Rudman. 2009. *Critical Multicultural Analysis of Children's Literature.* New York: Routledge.

Cole, Sonja. 2010. *Booktalking Around the World: Great Global Reads for Ages 9–14.* Santa Barbara, CA: Libraries Unlimited.

Cooper, Jewell, He, Ye, and Barbara Levin. 2011. *Developing Critical Cultural Competence: A Guide for 21st Century Educators.* Thousand Oaks, CA: Corwin/SAGE.

Diamant-Cohen, Betsy. 2010. *Early Literacy Programming en Español: Mother Goose on the Loose Programs for Bilingual Learners.* New York: Neal-Schuman.

Dresang, Eliza. 1999. *Radical Change: Books for Youth in a Digital Age.* New York: H. W. Wilson.

East, Kathy, and Rebecca L. Thomas. 2007. *Across Cultures: A Guide to Multicultural Literature for Children.* Westport, CT: Libraries Unlimited.

Farmer, Lesley. 2013. *Library Services for Youth with Autism Spectrum Disorders.* Chicago, IL: American Library Association.

Fox, Dana, and Kathy Short, eds. 2003. *Stories Matter: The Complexity of Cultural Authenticity in Children's Literature.* Urbana, IL: National Council of Teachers of English.

Freeman, Evelyn, and Barbara Lehman. 2001. *Global Perspectives in Children's Literature.* Boston: Allyn and Bacon.

Garner, Howard, and Katie Davis. 2013. *The App Generation: How Today's Youth Navigate Identity, Intimacy, and Imagination in a Digital World.* New Haven, CT: Yale University Press.

Gates, Pamela, and Dianne L. Hall Mark. 2006. *Cultural Journeys: Multicultural Literature for Children and Young Adults.* Lanham, MD: Scarecrow Press.

Gebel, Doris. 2006. *Crossing Boundaries with Children's Books.* Lanham, MD: Scarecrow Press.

Gopalakrishnan, Ambika. 2011. *Multicultural Children's Literature: A Critical Issues Approach.* Thousand Oaks, CA: SAGE.

Guernsey, Lisa. 2012. *Screen Time: How Electronic Media—From Baby Videos to Educational Software—Affects Your Young Child.* New York: Basic Books.

Guthrie, Dorothy Littlejohn. 2011. *Integrating African American Literature in the Library and Classroom.* Santa Barbara, CA: Libraries Unlimited.

Hadaway, Nancy, and Marian McKenna, eds. 2007. *Breaking Boundaries With Global Literature: Celebrating Diversity in K–12 Classrooms.* Newark, DE: International Reading Association.

Harrod, Kerol, and Carol Smallwood, eds. 2014. *Library Youth Outreach: 26 Ways to Connect with Children, Young Adults and Their Families.* Jefferson, NC: McFarland.

Henderson, Darwin, and Jill May. 2005. *Exploring Culturally Diverse Literature for Children and Adolescents: Learning to Listen in New Ways.* Boston: Allyn and Bacon.

Hernon, Peter, and Philip Calvert, eds. 2006. *Improving the Quality of Library Services for Students with Disabilities.* Westport, CT: Libraries Unlimited.

Klipper, Barbara. 2014. *Programming for Children and Teens with Autism Spectrum Disorder.* Chicago, IL: American Library Association.

Knowles, Liz, and Martha Smith. 2007. *Understanding Diversity Through Novels and Picture Books.* Westport, CT: Libraries Unlimited.

Kuharets, Olga. 2001. *Venture into Cultures: A Resource Book of Multicultural Materials and Programs.* 2nd ed. Chicago, IL: American Library Association.

Langer de Ramirez, Lori. 2006. *Voices of Diversity: Stories, Activities, and Resources for the Multicultural Classroom.* Columbus, OH: Pearson.

Larson, Jeanette. 2011. *El día de los niños/El día de los libros: Building a Culture of Literacy in Your Community Through Día.* Chicago, IL: American Library Association.

Lehman, Barbara, Evelyn Freeman, and Patricia Scharer. 2010. *Reading Globally, K–8: Connecting Students to the World Through Literature.* Thousand Oaks, CA: Corwin.

Lepman, Jella. 2002. *A Bridge of Children's Books: The Inspiring Autobiography of a Remarkable Woman.* Dublin, Ireland: The O'Brien Press.

MacDonald, Margaret Read. 2008. *Tell the World: Storytelling Across Language Barriers.* Westport, CT: Libraries Unlimited.

McGowan, Tara M. 2010. *The Kamishibai Classroom: Engaging Multiple Literacies Through the Art of "Paper Theater."* Santa Barbara, CA: Libraries Unlimited.

MacMillan, Kathy, and Christine Kirker. 2012. *Multicultural Storytime Magic.* Chicago, IL: American Library Association.

Marantz, Sylvia, and Ken Marantz. 2005. *Multicultural Picturebooks: Art for Illuminating Our World.* Lanham, MD: Scarecrow Press.

Martin, Michelle. 2004. *Brown Gold: Milestones of African American Children's Picture Books, 1845–2002.* New York: Routledge.

Naidoo, Jamie Campbell, ed. 2010. *Celebrating Cuentos: Promoting Latino Children's Literature and Literacy in Classrooms and Libraries.* Santa Barbara, CA: Libraries Unlimited.

Naidoo, Jamie Campbell. 2012. *Rainbow Family Collections: Selecting and Using Children's Books with Lesbian, Gay, Bisexual, Transgender, and Queer Content.* Santa Barbara, CA: Libraries Unlimited.

Naidoo, Jamie Campbell, and Sarah Park Dahlen, eds. 2013. *Diversity in Youth Literature: Opening Doors Through Reading*. Chicago: American Library Association.

Neuman, Susan B., and Donna C. Celano. 2012. *Giving Our Children a Fighting Chance: Poverty, Literacy and the Development of Information Capital*. New York: Teachers College Press.

Nichols, Joel. 2013. *iPads in the Library: Using Tablet Technology to Enhance Programs for All Ages*. Santa Barbara, CA: Libraries Unlimited.

Norton, Donna. 2012. *Multicultural Children's Literature: Through the Eyes of Many Children*. 4th ed. Boston: Pearson.

Pavonetti, Linda M., ed. 2011. *Bridges to Understanding: Envisioning the World Through Children's Books*. Lanham, MD: Scarecrow Press.

Schon, Isabel. 2009. *Recommended Books in Spanish for Children and Young Adults: 2004–2008*. Lanham, MD: Scarecrow Press.

Seale, Doris, and Beverly Slapin. 2005. *A Broken Flute: The Native Experience in Books for Children*. Walnut Creek, CA: AltaMira Press/Rowman & Littlefield Publishers.

Simon, Fran, and Karen Nemeth. 2012. *Digital Decisions: Choosing the Right Technology Tools for Early Childhood Education*. Lewisville, NC: Gryphon House.

Smallwood, Carol, and Kim Becnel, eds. 2013. *Library Services for Multicultural Patrons: Strategies to Encourage Library Use*. Jefferson, NC: McFarland.

Smith, Henrietta M., ed. 2009. *The Coretta Scott King Awards 1970–2009*. 4th ed. Chicago, IL: American Library Association.

Smolin, Lynn Atkinson, and Ruth A. Oswald, eds. 2011. *Multicultural Literature and Response: Affirming Diverse Voices*. Santa Barbara, CA: Libraries Unlimited.

Souto-Manning, Mariana. 2013. *Multicultural Teaching in the Early Childhood Classroom: Approaches, Strategies, and Tools, Preschool–2nd Grade*. New York: Teachers College Press, and Washington, DC: Association for Childhood Education International.

Stan, Susan. 2014. *Global Voices: Picture Books from Around the World*. Chicago: American Library Association.

Stan, Susan. 2002. *The World Through Children's Books*. Lanham, MD: Scarecrow Press.

Steiner, Stanley, and Peggy Hokom. 2001. *Promoting a Global Community Through Multicultural Children's Literature.* Englewood, CO: Libraries Unlimited.

Steiner-Adair, Catherine, and Teresa H. Barker. 2013. *The Big Disconnect: Protecting Childhood and Family Relationships in the Digital Age.* New York: Harper.

Stewart, Michelle Pagni, and Yvonne Atkinson, eds. 2009. *Ethnic Literary Traditions in American Children's Literature.* New York: Palgrave MacMillan.

Taylor-DiLeva, Kim. 2010. *Once Upon a Sign: Using American Sign Language to Engage, Entertain, and Teach All Children.* Santa Barbara, CA: Libraries Unlimited.

Treviño, Rose Zertuche. 2006. *The Pura Belpré Awards: Celebrating Latino Authors and Illustrators.* Chicago, IL: American Library Association.

Wadham, Tim. 2007. *Libros Escenciales: Building, Marketing, and Programming a Core Collection of Spanish Language Children's Materials.* New York: Neal-Schuman.

Webber, Desiree, Dee Corn, Elaine R. Harrod, Sandy Shropshire, Shereen Rasor, and Donna Norvell. 2013. *Travel the Globe: Story Times, Activities, and Crafts for Children.* Santa Barbara, CA: Libraries Unlimited.

York, Sherry. 2009. *Booktalking Authentic Multicultural Literature: Fiction and History for Young Readers.* Columbus, OH: Linworth.

Selected Articles

Agosto, Denise. 2008. "The Lubuto Library Project: As a Model of School Library Media Services for Disadvantaged Youth." *Knowledge Quest* 37(1): 38–42.

Al-Hazza, Tami Craft, and Katherine T. Butcher. 2008. "Building Arab Americans' Cultural Identity and Acceptance with Children's Literature." *The Reading Teacher* 62(3): 210–219.

Banks, Cheryl, Ellen Cole, and Linda Silver. 2006. "The Quest for Excellence in Jewish Children's Literature." *Judaica Librarianship* 12: 69–78.

Berry, John D. 2004. "White Privilege in Library Land." *Library Journal* 129(11): 50.

Blagojevic, Bonnie, Hilary Brumer, Sue Chevalier, Audrey O'Clair, and Karen Thomas. 2012. "Touch and Grow: Learning and Exploring Using Tablets." *Teaching Young Children* 6(1): 18–21.

Bleeker, Gerrit, Barbara Bleeker, and Catherine Rickbone. 2003. "Let's Talk About It: An Intergenerational Family Literacy Program." *Voice of Youth Advocates* 26(4): 288–290.

Casement, Rose. 2002. "Breaking the Silence: The Stories of Gay and Lesbian People in Children's Literature." *New Advocate* 15(3): 205–213.

Chen, Fu-jen, and Su-lin Yu. 2006. "Asian North-American Children's Literature About the Internment: Visualizing and Verbalizing the Traumatic Thing." *Children's Literature in Education* 37(2): 111–124.

Chen, S. 2002. "Asian American Literature in School Libraries." *Journal of Educational Media and Library Service* 39(3): 251–268.

Chick, Kay. 2008. "Fostering an Appreciation for all Kinds of Families: Picturebooks with Gay and Lesbian Themes." *Bookbird* 46(1): 15–22.

Dias-Mitchell, Laurie, and Elizabeth Harris. 2001. "Multicultural Mosaic: A Family Book Club." *Knowledge Quest* 29(4): 17–21.

Dresang, Eliza, Beth Patin, and Bowie Kotrla. 2014. "Cultivating Cultural Competence: Context, Culture, and Technology of a Global Reading Challenge." *iConference 2014 Proceedings* 643–648. doi:10.9776/14304.

Frostick, Cary Meltzer. 2009. "The Myth of Equal Access: Bridging the Gap with Diverse Patrons." *Children and Libraries* 7(3): 32–37.

Gangi, Jane M. 2005. "Inclusive Aesthetics and Social Justice: The Vanguard of Small, Multicultural Presses." *Children's Literature Association Quarterly* 30(3): 233–264.

Greenwalt, R. Toby. 2013. "Of Tinkers and Technology: Creative Digital Programming for Youth." *Public Libraries* 52(4): 18–20.

Higgins, Nicholas. 2013. "Family Literacy on the Inside." *Public Libraries* 52(1): 30–35.

Hughes-Hassell, Sandra, and Ernie J. Cox. 2010. "Inside Board Books: Representations of People of Color." *The Library Quarterly* 80(3): 211–230.

Huskey, Melynda. 2002. "Queering the Picture Book." *The Lion and the Unicorn* 26(1): 66–77.

Kuglin, Mandee. 2009. "Latino Outreach: Making Día a Fiesta of Family Literacy." *Children and Libraries* 7(3): 42–46.

McNair, Jonda. (2013). "I Never Knew There Were So Many Books About Us: Parents and Children Reading African American Children's Literature Together." *Children's Literature in Education* 44(3), 191–207.

Menkart, Deborah. 2006. "Heritage Months and Celebrations: Some Considerations." In *Beyond Heroes and Holidays,* ed. by Enid Lee, Deborah Menkart, and Margo Okazawa-Rey, 380–382. Washington DC: Network of Educators on the Americas.

Montiel-Overall, Patricia. 2009. "Cultural Competence: A Conceptual Framework for Library and Information Science Professionals." *The Library Quarterly* 79(2): 175–204.

Montiel-Overall, Patricia. 2008. "School Library Services in a Multicultural Society: The Need for Cultural Competence." In *School Library Services in a Multicultural Society,* ed. by P. Montiel-Overall and Donald C. Adcock, 3–7. Chicago: American Library Association.

Moreillon, Judi. 2013. "Building Bridges for Cultural Understanding: Cultural Literature Collection Development and Programming." *Children and Libraries* 11(2): 35–38.

Morgan, Hani. 2009. "Gender, Racial, and Ethnic Misrepresentation in Children's Books: A Comparative Look." *Childhood Education* 85(3):187–190.

Myers, Christopher. 2014. "The Apartheid of Children's Literature." *New York Times* (March 15). Accessed March 17, 2014, at http://www.nytimes.com/2014/03/16/opinion/sunday/the-apartheid-of-childrens-literature.html.

Myers, Walter Dean. 2014. "Where Are the People of Color in Children's Books?" *New York Times* (March 15). Accessed March 17, 2014, at http://www.nytimes.com/2014/03/16/opinion/sunday/where-are-the-people-of-color-in-childrens-books.html.

Naidoo, Jamie Campbell. 2013. "Over the Rainbow and Under the Radar: Library Services and Programs to LGBTQ Families." *Children and Libraries* 11(3), 34–40.

Naidoo, Jamie Campbell. 2012. "School and Public Library Services, Programs, and Collections for Diverse Youth in America." In *Youth-Serving Libraries in Japan, Russia, and the United States,* ed. by Lesley Farmer, 315–338. Lanham, MD: Scarecrow Press.

Nilsson, Nina. 2005. "How Does Hispanic Portrayal in Children's Books Measure Up After 40 Years? The Answer Is 'It Depends.'" *Reading Teacher* 58(6): 534–548.

O'Toole, Erin M. 2005. "Reading America Program Fosters Intergenerational Understanding in Chinese Immigrant Families." *Public Libraries* 44(6): 355–359.

Perkins, Mitali. 2009. "Straight Talk on Race: Challenging the Stereotypes in Kids' Books." *School Library Journal* 55(4): 28–32.

Reese, Debbi. 2013. "Resources and Kid Lit About American Indians." *School Library Journal* 59(11). Accessed February 28, 2014, at http://www.slj.com/2013/11/collection-development/focus-on-collection-development/resources-and-kid-lit-about-american-indians-focus-on/#_.

Rinaldi, Ann. 2003. "How Dare I Write Multicultural Novels?" *Book Links* 12(3): 31–33.

Rios-Balderrama, Sandra. 2006. "The Role of Cultural Competence in Creating a New Mainstream." *Colorado Libraries* 32(4): 3–8.

Roskos, Kathleen, Karen Burstein, Yi Shang, and Emily Gray. 2014. "Young Children's Engagement With E-Books at School: Does Device Matter?" *SAGE Open* 4(1): 1–9.

Rowell, Elizabeth. 2007. "Missing! Picture Books Reflecting Gay and Lesbian Families: Make the Curriculum Inclusive for All Children." *Young Children* 62(3): 24–30.

Schon, Isabel. 2006. "Opening New Worlds for Latino Children." *American Libraries* 37(5): 48–50.

Swartz, Patti Chapel. 2003. "Bridging Multicultural Education: Bringing Sexual Orientation into the Children's and Young Adult Literature Classrooms." *Radical Teacher* 66: 11–16.

Yamazaki, Akiko. 2002. "Why Change Names? On the Translation of Children's Books." *Children's Literature in Education* 33(1): 53–62.

Yokota, Junko. 2010. "Asian and Asian American Literature for Adolescents: What's Important for Librarians and Teachers to Know?" *Voice of Youth Advocates* 33(3): 214–215.

Online Resources

Collection Development Blogs, Recommended Lists, Critical Conversations About Diversity in Children's Literature

All Brown All Around: A Blog About Latinos in Children's and YA Books by Celia C. Perez
http://all-brown-all-around.blogspot.com/

American Indians in Children's Literature by Debbie Reese
http://americanindiansinchildrensliterature.blogspot.com/

Brown Bookshelf by Varian Johnson, Don Tate, Kelly Starling Lyons, Tameka Fryer Brown, Olugbemisola Rhuday-Perkovic, Gwendolyn Hooks, Crystal Allen, and Paula Chase-Hyman
http://thebrownbookshelf.com/

CBC Diversity by Children's Book Council
http://www.cbcdiversity.com

Children's Books by and About People of Color (Annual Statistics) by the Cooperative Children's Book Center, University of Wisconsin-Madison
http://ccbc.education.wisc.edu/books/pcstats.asp

Children's Peace Education Library by Rosemary Greiner and Margo Trombetta
http://www.childpeacebooks.org/cpb/

Community Toolbox: Cultural Competence in a Multicultural World by University of Kansas
http://ctb.ku.edu/en/table-of-contents/culture/cultural-competence

Cynthia Leitich Smith's Multicultural Children's Literature
http://www.cynthialeitichsmith.com/lit_resources/diversity/multicultural/multi_biblio.html

De Colores: The Raza Experience in Books for Children by Beverly Slapin et al.
http://decoloresreviews.blogspot.com

Gay-Themed Picture Books for Children by Patricia Sarles
    http://booksforkidsingayfamilies.blogspot.com/

GLBT Resources for Children: A Bibliography by the American Library
    Association
    http://www.ala.org/ala/mgrps/rts/glbtrt/popularresources/children.
        cfm

Global Reading by Robin Gibson
    http://globalreading.weebly.com/

Growing Up in the Americas: Books as Passports to Global
    Understanding for Children in the United States by Association of
    Library Services to Children
    http://www.ala.org/alsc/compubs/booklists/growingupwrld/
        GrowingUpAroundWorld

International Children's Digital Library by University of Maryland
    http://en.childrenslibrary.org/

Fire Escape by Mitali Perkins
    http://www.mitaliperkins.com/

Latinas 4 Latino Lit by Viviana Hurtado and Monica Olivera
    http://latinas4latinolit.org/

Open Book: Critical Discussions of Culture in Children's Media by Lee &
    Low Books
    http://blog.leeandlow.com/

People of Color Picture Books Project!
    http://pocpicturebooks.wikispaces.com/

Rainbow Rumpus by Laura Matanah
    http://www.rainbowrumpus.org/

Teaching for Change Themed Booklist of Social Justice Children's Titles
    http://bbpbooks.teachingforchange.org/best-recommended/booklist

World of Words: International Collection of Children's and Adolescent
    Literature by the University of Arizona
    http://wowlit.org/

The World Through Picture Books: Librarians' Favourite Books from
  Their Country by IFLA (the International Federation of Library
  Associations and Institutions) section Libraries for Children and
  Young Adults with support from partners IFLA section Literacy and
  Reading and IBBY (International Board on Books for Young People)
  http://www.ifla.org/node/6718

Cultural Literacy Programs

Bridging Cultures: Muslim Journeys by the National Endowment
  for the Humanities in collaboration with the American Library
  Association's Public Program Office
  http://bridgingcultures.neh.gov/muslimjourneys/
  http://www.programminglibrarian.org/muslimjourneys/

¡Colorín Colorado! by Reading Rockets
  http://www.colorincolorado.org/

Comienza en Casa/It Starts at Home by Maine Migrant Education
  Program and Mano en Mano/Hand in Hand
  www.manomaine.org/ComienzaEnCasa

Dai Dai Xiang Chuan: Bridging Generations, a Bag at a Time by Chinese
  American Librarians Association
  http://daidai.cala-web.org/

Global Reading Challenge by Terry Lason, Mary Palmer, and Sue Warner
  http://www.kpl.gov/kids/global-reading-challenge.aspx
  http://www.spl.org/audiences/children/global-reading-challenge
  http://womensvoicesforchange.org/tag/seattle-public-librarys-
    global-reading-challenge

Noche de Cuentos by REFORMA (the National Association to Promote
  Library and Information Services to Latinos and the Spanish-
  Speaking)
  http://nochedecuentos.org/

Official El dia de los niños/El dia de los libros (Day of the Child/Day of
  the Book) by the Association for Library Service to Children
  http://www.ala.org/dia

Programming Librarian by the American Library Association
   http://www.programminglibrarian.org/home.html

Reading Is Grand! Celebrating Grand-Families@Your Library by the
   Black Caucus of the American Library Association
   bcalareadingisgrand.weebly.com

Sister Libraries Program by the Libraries for Children and Young Adults
   Section of IFLA
   http://sisterlibraries.wordpress.com/

Talk Story: Sharing Stories, Sharing Culture by the American Indian
   Library Association (AILA) and the Asian Pacific American
   Librarians Association (APALA)
   http://talkstorytogether.org/

Digital Media Resources and Digital App Review Sources

APPitic: App Lists for Education
   http://www.appitic.com/

Best Apps for Kids
   http://bestappsforkids.com/

Children's Technology Review
   http://childrenstech.com/

Common Sense Media
   https://www.commonsensemedia.org/app-reviews

Digital Media and Learning Research Hub by the University of California
   Humanities Research Institute
   http://dmlhub.net

Digital Media Diet
   http://digitalmediadiet.com/

Digital Natives with a Cause by the Hivos Knowledge Programme
   http://www.hivos.net/Hivos-Knowledge-Programme/Themes/
      Digital-Natives-with-a-Cause

The Digital Shift by Library Journal
http://www.thedigitalshift.com/

Digital Storytime
http://digital-storytime.com/

Fred Rogers Center for Early Learning and Children's Media by Saint
Vincent College
http://www.fredrogerscenter.org/

Global Kids Online Leadership Program by Global Kids, Inc.
http://www.olpglobalkids.org

Joan Ganz Cooney Center: Advancing Children's Learning in a Digital
Age by Sesame Workshop
http://www.joanganzcooneycenter.org/

Learning in Hand by Tony Vincent
http://learninginhand.com/

Little eLit
http://littleelit.com

Teachers With Apps
http://teacherswithapps.com

Young Digital: Digital Research with Children and Young People by the
Centre for Research on Families and Relationships (CRFR) and the
Masters in Childhood Studies at the University of Edinburgh
http://www.youngdigital.net

Awards for Culturally Diverse Children's Literature

Amelia Bloomer Project (Feminist Literature)
Sponsored by: Feminist Task Force of the American Library
Association's Social Responsibilities Round Table
http://ameliabloomer.wordpress.com/about/

American Indian Youth Literature Award (American Indian Literature)
Sponsored by: American Indian Library Association
http://ailanet.org/activities/american-indian-youth-literature-award/

Américas Award (Latin American, Caribbean, or Latino Literature in the
U.S.)
Sponsored by: Consortium of Latin American Studies Programs
http://www4.uwm.edu/clacs/aa/index.cfm and http://claspprograms.
org

Arab American Book Award
Sponsored by: Arab American National Museum
http://www.arabamericanmuseum.org/bookaward

Asian Pacific American Literature Award
Sponsored by: Asian Pacific American Librarians Association
http://www.apalaweb.org/awards/literature-awards/

Astrid Lindgren Memorial Award (International Children's Literature)
Sponsored by: Swedish Arts Council
http://www.alma.se/en/

Ben-Yitzhak Award (Jewish Illustrator Award)
Sponsored by: The Israel Museum
http://www.imj.org.il/exhibitions/2010/Ben-Yitzhak/museum_
prize_eng.pdf

Books for Africa, Books from Africa (African Literature)
Sponsored by: International Board on Books for Young People
http://www.ibby.org/index.php?id=553

Carter G. Woodson Award (Literature Depicting Ethnicity in the U.S.)
Sponsored by: National Council for the Social Studies
http://www.socialstudies.org/awards/woodson

Children's Africana Book Award (African Literature)
Sponsored by: African Studies Association
http://www.africaaccessreview.org/aar/awards.html

Coretta Scott King Award (African American Authored Literature)
Sponsored by: American Library Association
http://www.ala.org/ala/mgrps/rts/emiert/cskbookawards/index.cfm

Dolly Gray Award (Literature on Children with Disabilities)
Sponsored by: Division on Autism and Developmental Disabilities,
Council for Exceptional Children
http://daddcec.org/Awards/DollyGrayAwards.aspx

Hans Christian Andersen Award (International Award for Children's Literature)
  Sponsored by: International Board on Books for Young People
  http://www.ibby.org/index.php?id=273

Jane Addams Children's Book Award (Literature Promoting Peace, Social Justice, World Community, and Equality of the Sexes.)
  Sponsored by: Jane Addams Peace Association and Women's International League for Peace and Freedom
  http://www.janeaddamspeace.org/jacba/

Lambda Literary Award (LGBTQ Literature)
  Sponsored by: Lambda Literary Foundation
  http://www.lambdaliterary.org/awards/

Middle East Book Award (Middle Eastern Literature)
  Sponsored by: Middle East Outreach Council
  http://www.meoc.us/meoc/book-awards

Mildred L. Batchelder Award (Literature translated into English)
  Sponsored by: Association for Library Service to Children
  http://www.ala.org/alsc/awardsgrants/bookmedia/batchelderaward

Notable Books for a Global Society (Global Children's Literature)
  Sponsored by: the International Reading Association
  http://clrsig.org/nbgs.php

Outstanding Books for Young People with Disabilities (Differently Able)
  Sponsored by: International Board on Books for Young People
  http://www.usbby.org/list_obypdl.html

Outstanding International Booklist (Literature Originally Published Outside the U.S. and Later Published by a U.S. Publisher)
  Sponsored by: United States Board on Books for Young People
  http://www.usbby.org/list_oibl.html

Pura Belpré Award (Latino Literature)
  Sponsored by: Association for Library Service to Children and REFORMA
  http://www.ala.org/alsc/awardsgrants/bookmedia/belpremedal

Schneider Family Book Award (Literature for Children with Disabilities)
    Sponsored by: Katherine Schneider and the American Library
        Association
    http://www.ala.org/awardsgrants/schneider-family-book-award

South Asia Book Award (South Asian Literature)
    Sponsored by: South Asia National Outreach Consortium
    http://www.sanoc.org/saba.html

Stonewall Children's and Young Adult Literature Award (LGBT
    Literature)
    Sponsored by: American Library Association
    http://www.ala.org/glbtrt/award

Sydney Taylor Award (Jewish Literature)
    Sponsored by: Association of Jewish Libraries
    http://www.jewishlibraries.org/main/Awards/
        SydneyTaylorBookAward.aspx

TD Canadian Children's Literature Award (Canadian Literature)
    Sponsored by: TD Bank Group and Canadian Children's Book
        Centre
    http://www.bookcentre.ca/awards/td_canadian_childrens_literature_
        award

Tomás Rivera Mexican-American Children's Book Award (Mexican-
    American Literature)
    Sponsored by: Texas State University College of Education
    http://www.education.txstate.edu/c-p/Tomas-Rivera-Book-Award-
        Project-Link.html

Awards for Children's Digital Apps

Appy Awards
    Sponsored by: Media Post Communications
    http://www.mediapost.com/appyawards/

Bologna Ragazzi Digital Award
    Sponsored by: The Bologna Children's Book Fair
    http://www.bookfair.bolognafiere.it/en/bolognaragazzi-digital-
        award/1034.html

Digital Book Awards
> *Sponsored by:* Digital Book World
> http://www.digitalbookworld.com/the-digital-book-awards/

iKids Award
> *Sponsored by:* KidsScreen
> http://ikidsawards.kidscreen.com/

Kids at Play Interactive (KAPi) Awards
> *Sponsored by:* Living in Digital Times and *Children's Technology Review*
> https://childrenstech.com/kapis.

Publishers and Distributors of Culturally Diverse Children's Books

Africa World Press
> http://www.africaworldpressbooks.com/servlet/StoreFront

Annick Press
> http://www.annickpress.com/

Arte Público Press/Piñata Books
> http://artepublicopress.uh.edu/arte-publico-wp/

Asia for Kids
> http://www.afk.com/

Asian American Curriculum Project
> http://www.asianamericanbooks.com/

August House
> http://www.augusthouse.com/

Bess Press
> http://besspress.com/

Boyds Mills Press
> https://www.boydsmillspress.com/

Children's Book Press (imprint of Lee & Low Books)
> http://www.childrensbookpress.org/

Cinco Puntos Press
    http://www.cincopuntos.com/

Clear Light Books
    http://www.clearlightbooks.com/

Del Sol
    http://www.delsolbooks.com/

Fifth House Publishers
    http://www.fifthhousepublishers.ca/

Groundwood Books
    http://www.groundwoodbooks.com/

Hoopoe Books
    http://www.hoopoekids.com/

Jump at the Sun (imprint of Hyperion)
    http://www.leibowstudios.com/webdevelop/hyperion/jump/index.
        html

Just Us Books
    http://justusbooks.com/

Kane Miller
    http://www.kanemiller.com/

Kar-Ben Publishing
    http://www.karben.com/

Lectorum
    http://www.lectorum.com/

Lee & Low Books
    http://www.leeandlow.com/

Milet
    http://www.milet.com/

NorthSouth Books
    http://northsouthbooks.wordpress.com/

Oyate
> http://www.oyate.org/

Pan Asian Publications
> http://www.panap.com/

Santillana USA
> http://www.santillanausa.com/

Second Story Press
> http://secondstorypress.ca/list/children

Shen's Books (imprint of Lee & Low Books)
> http://www.shens.com/

Tamarind Books
> http://www.tamarindbooks.co.uk/

Theytus Books
> http://www.theytus.com/

Tilbury House Publishers
> http://www.tilburyhouse.com/

Tulika Books
> http://www.tulikabooks.com/

Two Lives Publishing
> http://twolivesbooks.wordpress.com/

Woodbine House
> http://www.woodbinehouse.com/

Specialized Periodicals Exploring Diversity in Children's Literature and in Educational Settings

Book Bird: A Journal of International Children's Literature
> http://www.ibby.org/index.php?id=276

International Research in Children's Literature
> http://www.irscl.com/ircl.html

Jeunesse: Young People, Texts, Cultures
  http://jeunessejournal.ca/index.php/yptc

Rethinking Schools
  http://www.rethinkingschools.org/index.shtml

Skipping Stone: An International Multicultural Magazine
  http://www.skippingstones.org/

Teaching Tolerance
  http://www.tolerance.org/

Library and Literacy Professional Organizations Dedicated to Culturally Diverse Groups

American Indian Library Association (AILA)
  http://www.ailanet.org/

American Library Association's Ethnic and Multicultural Information
  Exchange Round Table (EMIERT)
  http://www.ala.org/ala/mgrps/rts/emiert/index.cfm

American Library Association's GLBT Round Table (GLBTRT)
  http://www.ala.org/ala/mgrps/rts/glbtrt/index.cfm

American Library Association's Office for Diversity
  http://www.ala.org/ala/aboutala/offices/diversity/index.cfm

Asian Pacific American Librarians Association (APALA)
  http://www.apalaweb.org/

Association of Jewish Libraries (AJL)
  http://www.jewishlibraries.org/main/

Black Caucus of the American Library Association (BCALA)
  http://www.bcala.org/

Chinese American Librarians Association (CALA)
  http://www.cala-web.org/

Diversity Librarian's Network
  http://diversitylibrariansnetwork.blogspot.com/

International Board on Books for Young People (IBBY)
http://www.ibby.org/

International Federation of Library Associations and Institutions (IFLA)
http://www.ifla.org/

National Library Service for the Blind and Physically Handicapped (NLS)
http://www.loc.gov/nls/

REFORMA (The National Association to Promote Library and
Information Services to Latinos and the Spanish-Speaking)
http://www.reforma.org/

Index

A

About the Author

DR. JAMIE CAMPBELL NAIDOO is an endowed assistant professor at the University of Alabama School of Library and Information Studies and director/founder of the National Latino Children's Literature Conference. He teaches and researches in the areas of early childhood literacy, culturally diverse children's literature, and library services to Latino families. He is active in REFORMA and has chaired both the Pura Belpré and Américas Award committees. He is also the editor of *Celebrating Cuentos: Promoting Latino Children's Literature and Literacy in Classrooms and Libraries* (Libraries Unlimited, 2011) and author of *Rainbow Family Collections: Selecting and Using Children's Books with Lesbian, Gay, Bisexual, Transgender, and Queer Content* (Libraries Unlimited, 2012).